"Hip-Hop is as diverse as life."

Blake Harrison & Alexander Rappaport

Flocabulary

The Hip-hop approach to SAT-Level Vocabulary Building

Blake Harrison and Alexander Rappaport

Foreword by Dr. Ann Marie Mulready, PhD

CIDER MILL
PRESS

BOOK
PUBLISHERS

Kennebunkport, ME

∴ Flocabulary:
The Hip-hop approach to SAT-Level Vocabulary Building

ISBN: 1-933662-14-X

This book may be ordered by mail from the publisher. Please include $3.50 for postage and handling.
Please support your local bookseller first!

Books published by Cider mill Press Book Publishers are available at special discounts for bulk purchases in the United States by corporations, institutions, and other organizations. For more information, please contact the publisher.

Cider Mill Press Book Publishers
"Where good books are ready for press"
12 Port Farm Road
Kennebunkport, Maine 04046

Visit us on the web!
www.cidermillpress.com

Design by: Katherine Benedict
Printed in China

1 2 3 4 5 6 7 8 9 0
First Edition

Table of Contents

Acknowledgements

We want to give a huge thank-you to everybody who helped us along the way. A Dictionary and a Microphone never would have been possible without you. You gave us your comments, laughed with us, gave us love.

Extra-big thanks to: Dr. Ann Marie Mulready, Erena Shimoda, Jen Swanson, Stefanie Gold, Tony Porter and Tim Lukas at Blink Music, BZ Lewis at Studio 132, Dee1R, Mr. Black Satin, Afro DZ ak, Ed Boyer, Isaac Brody, Joe DeMatteo, and Pedro Peterson. Special thanks to: John Whalen, Buz Teacher, Liz McArthur, Bryony Gagan, Herb Rappaport, Steve and Heather, Lee Chazen, Brett Hodus, Kathleen Mulready, Amanda and Matt Dobbins, Devon and Tessa, Margaret Rappaport, Ziki Dekel and everybody at Sparknotes.com, and all the folks who signed the guestbook or who checked out our first four tracks. Thank-you!

Foreword

The psychological literature is replete with studies on the positive impact of rhythm, rhyme, and melody on memory and verbal learning.* Rhythm, rhyme, and melody, when embedded in a learning task, significantly increase the retention of material in long-term memory. Furthermore, researchers at Dartmouth are beginning to understand the biological supports for these strong connections. The musical pathway in the brain, the auditory cortex, continues to operate even when the music has stopped.

Scientific comprehension aside, most of us intuitively understand the power of music and poetry. Much of our early academic, social, and emotional learning is developed with rhythm, rhyme, and melody. We are introduced to academics with, "One, two, buckle my shoe" and singing the ABCs. Our poetic and musical pasts also embed more complex aspects of language. "Like a diamond in the sky" makes simile and metaphor meaningful, "monkey see-monkey do" conveys a social message, and lines like ". . . so many children, she didn't know what to do" develop humor and irony. In the emotional realm, an old lullaby can still soothe us and the babies who are rocked to sleep every night. And melody, beautiful or annoying, can become stuck in our heads.

Thus far, it's been difficult for teachers beyond the primary years of schooling to take advantage of the power of music and poetry as tools for learning. From my own experience as a high school English teacher and elementary and secondary language arts consultant, materials aimed at taking advantage of music's impact on learning are viewed as simplistic and silly by both teachers and students. With respect to vocabulary development–highly correlated to academic achievement and SAT scores–there is still little beyond drill and kill, fill in the blank, and look it up in the dictionary. Generations of teachers know that these exercises are motivation killers, and the research tells us they are not very effective with long-term vocabulary acquisition.

Unlike other vocabulary programs, Flocabulary harnesses the powerful forces of rhythm, rhyme, and music and motivates using the adolescent's own musical culture. And it does that in a meaningful way. Words are grouped thematically, creating a context by which definitions are more meaningful. These definitions are incorporated right into the lyrics of the songs, making it easier for students to learn vocabulary in unique contexts. And Flocabulary uses hip-hop, an increasingly popular musical genre that combines music, rhythm, and rhyme to socially and academically engage students with what they're learning in a way that other programs and courses don't. Most of all, it contributes fun to the learning process. After all, most of us did not dread another round of the ABCs.

–Dr. Ann Marie Mulready, PhD

*See:

Deutsch, D. 1972. Music and memory. <u>Psychology Today</u> 12:87{-}119.

Gardner, H. <u>Multiple Intelligences: The Theory in Practice.</u> New York: Basic Books, 1993.

Gfeller, K. 1983. Musical mnemonics as an aid to retention with normal and learning disabled students. <u>Journal of Music Therapy</u> 20(4):179{-}89.

Glazner, M. 1976. Intonation grouping and related words in free recall. <u>Journal of Verbal Learning and Verbal Behavior</u> 15:85{-}92.

Jalongo, M. and K. Bromley. 1984. Developing linguistic competence through song. <u>Reading Teacher</u> 37(9):840{-}45.

Serafine, M., R. Crowder, and B. Repp. 1984. Integration of melody and test in memory for songs. <u>Cognition</u> 16(3):285{-}303.

Staples, S. 1968. A paired-associates learning task utilizing music as the mediator: An exploratory study. <u>Journal of Music Therapy</u> 5(2):53{-}57.

Chapter 1: What is Flocabulary?

Welcome to Flocabulary!

Flocabulary fuses hip-hop music with vocabulary words and their definitions to make learning vocabulary easy and engaging. This CD/workbook package, A Dictionary and a Microphone, defines five hundred SAT-level words in eleven songs (roughly forty-five per song) and contains a bonus math track.

The workbook is divided into twelve sections that correspond to songs on the CD. Each chapter contains: lyrics, definitions (in addition to the definitions within the lyrics), a synonym matching exercise, ten multiple-choice sentence completion questions, and a short reading comprehension exercise.

Why does it work?

Flocabulary is mnemonic-laced rap music. Rap music is so easy to memorize in itself because it is based in rhyming, and using rhyme is one of the most effective memorization strategies. Just think about it: how many songs do you have memorized? For more on mnemonics, visit www.flocabulary.com/why.

How do I use Flocabulary?

A Dictionary and a Microphone will not single-handedly prepare you for the SAT. You should familiarize yourself with the exam, learn some strategies, and take practice tests before you sit down to take the test. You can find a list of the best SAT resources (most of which are free) online at www.flocabulary.com/sat.

A Dictionary and a Microphone helps with the vocabulary portion of your SAT preparation, and an extensive vocabulary is crucial to doing well on the SAT. The Critical Reading Section and the new Writing Section both have questions that target your vocabulary, and part of your grade for the essay is based on the appropriate use of challenging vocabulary words. So don't just memorize definitions; use these words in your life and on the test!

Online resources

Flocabulary is much more than this CD/workbook. We have lots of free online resources for you, including:

A figurative language guide, which has definitions and examples of figurative language:
www.flocabulary.com/hiphoplanguage

Writing tips that are easy-to-understand pointers for better writing:
www.flocabulary.com/writing

Printable flashcards for all the words:
www.flocabulary.com/flashcards

SAT tips, hints, and questions from students:
www.flocabulary.com/board

Study guide

While the way you use A Dictionary and a Microphone is ultimately up to you, we offer a guide on how to use the CD/workbook most effectively to expand your vocabulary. Here are the steps to follow:

1. Listen for content. Strap on some headphones, cue up the first track--Transformation–on your CD player, and open this workbook to the Transformation chapter. Play the song and follow along with the lyrics. Just as with most pieces of fiction writing, each Flocabulary track has a narrator, a

central theme, and plenty of examples of figurative language. Try to identify the narrator (is it a sun-loving student, an irreverent party-crasher?), the tone the narrator is using, the central theme, and a few examples of figurative language. To check your answers, turn to Chapter 3 for the Song Guide.

2. Listen for vocabulary words. Play the song again. This time make sure that you understand the meaning of each vocabulary word in the rap. If you hear a word whose definition isn't clear to you from the lyrics of the song, circle the word in the lyrics with a pencil. When the song is finished, look up those words you've circled in the right-hand column, next to the lyrics.

3. Memorize. Now it's time to play the song enough times to memorize the lyrics. Go somewhere where you can rap along and you won't be bothering anyone. Play the song and rap out loud while reading along. It shouldn't take too many repetitions before you've got the entire song down.

4. Hammer in the definitions (optional). Use the printable flashcards online (www.flocabulary.com/flashcards) or make your own to hammer in the definitions of the words. If there are certain words you are always missing, go back and memorize that portion of the song again, or write your own rhyming lines to remember the definition.

5. Test yourself. Once you've memorized the words, you can test your knowledge by completing the exercises in the workbook. Either test yourself after each chapter, or after you've memorized a few of the songs. The answers are located in the back of the book.

6. Repeat with each track. And have fun.

Chapter 2: The Songs

Transformation

Word Bank

Myopic
Ratiocinate
Render
Recapitulate
Loquacious
Verbose
Gregarious
Elocution
Circumlocution
Cogent
Seminal
Meritorious
Redact
Placate
Tedious
Tome
Peruse
Entomology
Ostracize
Pariah
Persevere
Latent

Burgeon
Diligent
Paragon
Commodious
Clairvoyant
Cosmopolitan
Vast
Voluminous
Recalcitrant
Exorbitant
Extravagant
Colossus
Synopsis
Cadence
Cavort
Boisterous
Daft
Deft

The transformation of bookworms
into hip-hop icons,
a dictionary and a microphone,
a dictionary and a mic.

Now this here's a story for
the fellows and ladies,
sporting pocket protectors and
socket inspectors and marking their vectors,
glasses thick,
they're **myopic**, short-sighted,
they can't see the crumbs on their lips.
They don't say the word think,
they say "**ratiocinate**."
They don't **render** repeat,
they say **recapitulate**.
When they speak they're
wordy and **loquacious**,
verbose and **gregarious**,
so many words it's hilarious.
They study **elocution**,
the art of public speaking,
but they talk in **circumlocutions**,
indirect language.
They're **recalcitrant**,
defiant, and unapologetic.
Write an essay on
Shakespeare for extra credit.
So **cogent** and smart
that it changes the field,
it's **seminal** and original.
Their **meritorious** work always deserves merit,
they revise and **redact** their papers, they edit.
They **placate** their parents,
soothe them out,
by always getting good grades
and never leaving the house.
To them homework is never **tedious**,

myopic (adj.) - short-sighted

ratiocinate (v.) - to think, contemplate
render (v.) - to say, or to make
recapitulate (v) - to repeat, reiterate

loquacious (adj.) - talkative
verbose (adj.) - wordy
gregarious (adj.) - sociable
elocution (n.) - the art of public speaking

circumlocution (n.) - indirect language

recalcitrant (adj.) - defiant

cogent (adj.) - intelligent, viable

seminal (adj.) - original, ground-breaking
meritorious (adj.) - deserving of praise or merit
redact (v.) - to revise, edit
placate (v.) - to soothe, appease

tedious (adj.) - boring, dull

dull and boring, they're never snoring or
yawning
they're working evening and morning.
They have **tomes**, large books
in their homes, which they read and **peruse**
when
they're talking to you on the phone.
They know about Pokemon,
Everquest, insects, **entomology**,
Dungeons and Dragons, and chess.

The transformation of bookworms
into hip-hop icons,
a dictionary and a microphone,
a dictionary and a mic.

Now if you've ever felt left out and
ostracized, like a **pariah**,
try Flocabulary Cereal with fiber.
We put the k in Outkast,
persevere, persist, and outlast,
we're part of this complete breakfast.
Your **latent** skills, hidden skills,
will **burgeon** and blossom,
after one bite, it'll be awesome.
If you're following the serving suggestions
diligently, carefully,
you'll be more hip-hop than Run D.M.C.
You'll be the **paragon** of animals,
the model of perfection,
blowing up the session like a
Mormon on a mission.
You're house will be more roomy and
commodious,
you'll be more **clairvoyant** than
Nostradamus.
Gaze into your crystal ball, more
cosmopolitan than Carrie Bradshaw,

tome (n.) - a large book
peruse (v.) - to examine carefully

entomology (n.) - the study of insects

ostracize (v.) - to exclude from a community
pariah (n.) - an outcast

persevere (v.) - to persist, remain constant

latent (adj.) - present but hidden
burgeon (v.) - to come forth, blossom

diligent (adj.) - careful, showing care

paragon (n.) - model of perfection

commodious (adj.) - spacious, roomy
clairvoyant (adj.) - able to see and detect
things that others cannot

cosmopolitan (adj.) - worldly, sophisticated

with her humongous, **vast**, **voluminous**,
exorbitant, extensive,
extravagant collection of shoes, sophisticated
shoes.
You'll be larger than a **colossus**,
Tony Danza will ask you who the boss is.
Summarize in a speech and give a **synopsis**.
Your speech will have that **cadence**,
that rhythm, progression of sound,
that makes people **cavort**, dance, and get
down.
You used to have a **boisterous** loud laugh,
people used to
think of you as crazy and **daft**.
Now you're so **deft** and skilled you got mass
appeal,
people crowd around you like Jesus eating his
last meal.

The transformation of bookworms
into hip-hop icons,
a dictionary and a microphone,
a dictionary and a mic.

vast (adj.) - enormous, immense
voluminous (adj.) - large, ample
exorbitant (adj.) - excessive
extravagant (adj.) - excessive, over-the-top
colossus (n.) - an enormous structure

synopsis (n.) - a summary
cadence (n.) - rhythm

cavort (v.) – to prance, dance about

boisterous (adj.) - loud, energetic

daft (adj.) - insane, foolish
deft (adj.) - skilled, adept

Do You Remember?

Synonym Matching: In the space provided, write the letter of the synonym on the right that corresponds to the word on the left.

1. Placate _____   A. Defiant
2. Ratiocinate _____   B. Appease
3. Tedious _____   C. Adept
4. Tome _____   D. Prance
5. Recalcitrant _____   E. Book
6. Redact _____   F. Think
7. Burgeon _____   G. Summary
8. Synopsis _____   H. Blossom
9. Deft _____   I. Boring
10. Cavort _____   J. Revise

Sentence Completion: Each sentence below has one blank, indicating that something has been omitted. Beneath the sentence are five words labeled A through E. Choose the word that, when inserted in the sentence, best fits the meaning of the sentence as a whole.

1. There was a talkative girl in my English class who called herself "Chatty Cathy"; she was easily the most _____ girl in school and proud of it.

A) Taciturn
B) Sagacious
C) Ribald
D) Confounding
E) Loquacious

2. My lawyer encouraged me to carefully _____ the cell phone contract before signing.

A) Disregard
B) Rebuke
C) Peruse
D) Ascertain
E) Incinerate

3. After reading Kafka's Metamorphosis, in which the protagonist morphs into a cockroach, I became a fanatical student of _____.

A) Ornithology
B) Botany
C) Ecology
D) Scientology
E) Entomology

4. Always calm under pressure, Pharell won the debate based on his _____ arguments and perfectly structured rebuttals.

A) Vacuous
B) Tenuous
C) Cogent
D) Boisterous
E) Quixotic

5. The four years spent camping on the polar ice cap became worthwhile when Dr. Schnoo was awarded a Nobel Prize for completing _____ research on penguin bathing habits.

A) Antediluvian
B) Discursive
C) Ominous
D) Frivolous
E) Seminal

6. Abraham Lincoln, John F. Kennedy, and Bill Clinton are known as commanding presidents and master _____, often mesmerizing audiences with the spoken word.

A) Artisans
B) Elocutionists
C) Citizens
D) Denizens
E) Anarchists

7. Sometimes used-car salesmen have a way of speaking in _____; I wish they'd just tell it like it is!

A) Chorus
B) Paradoxes
C) Maledictions
D) Circumlocutions
E) Paradigms

8. Maria loved being a teacher for those moments when she discovered a(n) _____ talent in one of her most timid students.

A) Latent
B) Obvious
C) Fortuitous
D) Lucid
E) Malleable

9. The Bentley is the _____ of luxury vehicles, and a staple for Hollywood's elite.

A) Doppelganger
B) Medley
C) Paragon
D) Reservoir
E) Solvent

10. Just because Tessa predicted that J. Lo and Ben Affleck would break up doesn't make her _____; that was a pretty predictable outcome!

A) Obdurate
B) Clairvoyant
C) Vivacious
D) Vapid
E) Trite

Reading Comprehension: Read the passage below and answer the questions based on the text.

The most popular kid in school was a rapper named Theo. He was the paragon of popularity at Attleboro High; so deft with a microphone that it rendered people silent with awe. He had a colossal entourage that faithfully followed him from class to class, and he dressed in the most cosmopolitan fashions. But if you asked Theo, he would have told you that he felt ostracized by one particular group: the chess club. Then, one day, Theo wasn't in school. When he came in the next day, something had changed. He wore thick, black-rimmed glasses. When someone asked Theo why, he said, "Why don't you ratiocinate for a minute? Could it be because I'm myopic? Oh, and call me Theodore." Needless to say, the school didn't know what to do. Theodore stopped rapping and joined the debate team to study elocution. He joined the Ant-Lovers Club to study entomology, and he walked the hallways with oversized Dungeons and Dragons tomes under his arm. There is a happy ending, however, for the chess club no longer treated him like a pariah. They welcomed Theodore as one of their own.

1. Which of the following does not attest or contribute to Theo's popularity early on in the passage?

(A) He was a skilled rapper.
(B) He had many followers.
(C) He wore sophisticated clothes.
(D) He was mostly silent.
[(E) is missing?]

2. Which of the following most closely describes the reaction of the school in general to Theo's transformation?

(A) Hatred
(B) Bewilderment
(C) Appreciation
(D) Apprehension
(E) Disgust

Shakespeare Is Hip-Hop

Word Bank

Quotidian	Perfunctory	Subsist
Fey	Mandatory	Notoriety
Gay	Flaccid	Blandish
Pervasive	Flabbergasted	Flattery
Douse	Forage	Innocuous
Pliable	Licentious	Neonate
Neologism	Lewd	Incessant
Commendable	Profane	Narrate
Profuse	Fortuitous	Flout
Abundant	Serendipity	Pedagogue
Radiant	Abrogate	Buffet
Fecund	Algid	
Forestall	Brumal	
Poach	Hiemal	
Fetter	Impecunious	
Figurative	Hapless	
Myriad	Hiatus	
Plethora	Gregarious	
Sacrosanct	Inquisitor	
Fabricate	Iniquity	
Facile	Goad	
Fatuous	Ingenious	

The foundation of the English language is wordplay. **Quotidian**, everyday people making it stay, inventing synonyms like magical and **fey**, happy and **gay**, but the last example will show you that meanings can change. Language is **pervasive**, spreading throughout, like perfume you **doused** or dripped on your blouse when you stepped in the house. Language is **pliable**, bendable, and amendable. **Neologism** is inventing new words, that's **commendable**, deserving of praise. We're more **profuse** than the rays, more **abundant** than sunrays on the **radiant** days. Language offers so many choices it's fertile and **fecund**, flipping free-styling flows for all my folks on the weekend. To **forestall** and delay the approach of Monday, approaching. We hunt illegally so we're **poaching**. They can't **fetter** our words, chain them or restrain them, we're liberating people, like Toussaint did the Haitians. You'll find **figurative** language in rap and Shakespeare, symbolic meaning, similes and metaphors in there. I love the English language, it has so many words, **myriad** words, a **plethora** of nouns and verbs.

Hip-hop is Shakespeare,
and Shakespeare is hip-hop . . .

A dictionary's not sacred, not **sacrosanct**, no it's more like a bank, put stuff in and take it out again. If I **fabricate** a word like hiphopperoperey, in fifty years you might find that word on the SAT. Wordplay is **facile**, every three-year-old does it, saying mo-mo for motorcycle, cuzy for cousin. It's **fatuous**, silly, and foolish, to think that if you say a

quotidian (adj.) - daily, everyday
fey (adj.) - magical
gay (adj.) - happy, cheery, or homosexual

pervasive (adj.) - inclined to spread throughout
douse (v.) - to drench, saturate
pliable (adj.) - flexible, bendable
neologism (n.) - the creation of new words, or a new word
commendable (adj.) - worthy of praise
profuse (adj.) - abundant, lavish, prolific
abundant (adj.) - in great numbers
radiant (adj.) - bright, beaming
fecund (adj.) - fertile, fruitful
forestall (v.) - to delay, impede
poach (v.) - to hunt or fish illegally
fetter (v.) - to restrain, chain, tie

figurative (adj.) - symbolic

myriad (adj.) - many, of great numbers
plethora (n.) - a great number, an abundance

sacrosanct (adj.) - sacred, holy

fabricate (v.) - to invent, make up, concoct

facile (adj.) - easy

fatuous (adj.) - silly, foolish

word incorrectly then you are stupid. Some people study vocab in a manner that's **perfunctory**, showing little enthusiasm like it was **mandatory**, not optional. Me without a mic is like a plant without water. It grows limp and **flaccid**, I get **flabbergasted** and astounded. I **forage** through this language like I rummage for food. I might find words that are rude, crude, **licentious**, or **lewd**, words that are vulgar, indecent, and **profane**, but even those dirty words have a specific meaning. Sometimes I'm **fortuitous**, lucky, and fortunate, I find a word like fortuitous on my first pick. That's **serendipity**, oddly good luck, like finding a buck, or a bullet coming at you when you duck.

Hip-hop is Shakespeare,
and Shakespeare is hip-hop . . .

Some cats try to abolish and **abrogate** Fahrenheit, switch it over to centigrade, but a cold flow by any other name would be as chill, as **algid,** as frigid, as cold, as **brumal**, as **hiemal**, as wintry as snow. But hush, what wind from yonder window blows, it's the sweet smell of synonyms, open your ears for them, yo, 'cause here they go: A poor cat: an **impecunious** feline. A **hapless hiatus**: an unlucky break in time. A sociable questioner: a **gregarious inquisitor**, the kind of man you'd invite to supper or dinner. The seven deadly sins: seven lethal **iniquities**. He urged the clever man fast: **goaded** the **ingenious** man quickly. He lives in infamy: **subsists** in **notoriety**. To coax with compliments: **blandish** with **flattery**. The harmless baby: the **innocuous neonate**. Tell a never-ending

perfunctory (adj.) - showing little enthusiasm, done as duty
mandatory (adj.) - required, not optional
flaccid (adj.) - limp
flabbergasted (adj.) - astounded, stupefied
forage (v.) - to rummage, scavenge, graze for food
licentious (adj.) - immoral, lewd
lewd (adj.) - vulgar, offensive, rude
profane (adj.) - indecent, blasphemous
fortuitous (adj.) - lucky, occurring by chance
serendipity (n.) - the act of finding things not sought, luck

abrogate (v.) - to abolish, often by authority
algid (adj.) - frigid, cold
brumal (adj.) - wintry, relating to winter
hiemal (adj.) - wintry, relating to winter
impecunious (adj.) - excessively poor
hapless (adj.) - unlucky
hiatus (n.) - an interruption in continuity, a break
gregarious (adj.) - sociable, outgoing
inquisitor (n.) - someone who asks questions or makes an inquiry
iniquity (n.) - a wicked act, a sin
goad (v.) - to urge, provoke
ingenious (adj.) - marked by special intelligence
subsist (v.) - to live, exist
notoriety (n.) - infamy, known in bad regard
blandish (v.) - to coax through flattery
flattery (n.) - compliments, sycophancy
innocuous (adj.) - harmless
neonate (n.) - a newborn baby

story: you **incessantly narrate**. Don't ignore your teacher: don't **flout** your **pedagogue**. Don't **buffet** your canine: don't beat your dog.

incessant (adj.) - without interruption
narrate (v.) - to tell a story
flout (v.) - to scorn, ignore, show contempt for
pedagogue (n.) - a schoolteacher
buffet (v.) - to hit or strike

Do You Remember?

Synonym Matching: In the space provided, write the letter of the synonym on the right that corresponds to the word on the left.

1. Fey _____
2. Pliable _____
3. Profuse _____
4. Fecund _____
5. Fetter _____
6. Flaccid _____
7. Abrogate _____
8. Gregarious _____
9. Innocuous _____
10. Flout _____

A. Limp
B. Ignore
C. Abundant
D. Harmless
E. Bendable
F. Fertile
G. Sociable
H. Magical
I. Restrain
J. Abolish

Sentence Completion: Each sentence below has one blank, indicating that something has been omitted. Beneath the sentence are five words labeled A through E. Choose the word that, when inserted in the sentence, best fits the meaning of the sentence as a whole.

1. Brushing one's teeth should be a _____ habit.
A) Rare
B) Tedious
C) Quotidian
D) Laborious
E) Wanton

2. Hip-hop is responsible for a handful of recent _____, bringing forth words like "bling-bling" and "foshizzle."
A) Quandaries
B) Pedagogies
C) Crescendos
D) Paradigms
E) Neologisms

3. As the legend goes, Sisyphus was _____ to a giant boulder, which he had to roll up a mountainside over and over again.
A) Fettered
B) Servile
C) Tattooed
D) Absconded
E) Inured

4. It was surprising that the actress accepted the Oscar in a manner that was so nonchalant and _____.
A) Pert
B) Sanguine
C) Repentant
D) Precocious
E) Perfunctory

5. This rude guy named Stanley was ejected from the stands at the basketball game for taunting the opposing team and making _____ gestures with his hands.
A) Saccharine
B) Lewd
C) Sacrosanct
D) Rancid
E) Lithe

6. The fact that I found a rare, 1924 penny in a pair of thrift-store pants is a great example of the recent _____ in my life.
A) Enmity
B) Apathy
C) Serendipity
D) Complacency
E) Ennui

7. The impoverished Favelas outside of Rio de Janeiro are among the most _____ urban communities in the world.
A) Gaudy
B) Opulent
C) Sprawling
D) Venerated
E) Impecunious

8. Wild Bill Jones has a remarkable diet; he _____ entirely on berries and bark.
A) Modulates
B) Transgresses
C) Procures
D) Subsists
E) Palliates

9. It was supposed to be a conversation, but Muhammad was talking so _____ that Willie couldn't get a single word in edgewise.
A) Occasionally
B) Licentiously
C) Sporadically
D) Succinctly
E) Incessantly

10. When I took my date to the county fair, all she wanted to do was play the game where you _____ the plastic gophers with a small rubber bat.
A) Buffet
B) Venerate
C) Placate
D) Truncate
E) Yoke

Reading Comprehension: Read the passage below and answer the questions based on the text.

Manny and Mykala crouched behind one of the myriad statues that dotted the prince's lawn. The day was radiant but brumal, and the two had to brace themselves against the swift, algid wind that came rolling in from the sea. But they were fortuitous: after just fifteen minutes of waiting, a giant wild turkey came strutting out of the underbrush. Three months earlier, the prince had abrogated hunting, arguing that what was once a plethora of wildlife had dwindled far enough. So Manny and Mykala were poaching, flouting the prince's decree like Romeo and Juliet flouted the wishes of their parents. It was with beating hearts that they took aim at the hapless, oblivious bird.

1. In the passage above, what best describes why the wild turkey is "hapless"?
(A) He is on the prince's land.
(B) He is about to be shot.
(C) He is vaguely aware of what is going on.
(D) He is poaching.
(E) He is giant.

2. Which of the following would best describe the weather mentioned in the passage?
(A) Rainy and hot
(B) Cloudless and cold
(C) Humid and breezy
(D) Cloudy and windy
(E) Stormy and freezing

Word Bank

Fortify
Dictate
Diminutive
Goad
Lachrymose
Obsequious
Laud
Sycophant
Officious
Abide
Punctilious
Propriety
Amble
Scurrilous
Inimical
Trek
Malevolent
Malicious
Truculent
Pugnacious
Belligerent
Accost

Invective
Timorous
Circumspect
Prudent
Nefarious
Petulance
Repudiate
Accede
Accommodating
Poised
Masticate
Spurious
Abate
Abase
Laceration
Altercation
Mediate
Arbitrator
Restitution
Retaliation
Retribution
Umbrage

Upbraid
Berate
Atone
Benevolent
Bereft
Concede

If you don't stand strong you get knocked around, **fortify** like a fort or else you'll fall down. Eventually every living thing will fall into the sea, how could I let someone else **dictate** who I'm gonna be?

fortify (v.) - to strengthen

dictate (v.) - to pronounce, command, prescribe

I know this cat named Carlos, we called him Carlito, the poor baby brother had a really small ego. **Diminutive** in size, 4 foot 9, if you provoked or **goaded** him, it would bring tears to his eyes. He lived a **lachrymose** life, very tearful, and careful not to be out too late or he'd get an earful. We'd go out with friends, Carlos was **obsequious**, submissive, crawling on his hands and knees for us. "Hey guys, can I hold the door? Let me fold your napkin." He **lauded** and applauded us, he was always clapping, a **sycophant**, a kiss-up, on the court a mismatch. When you offer services and they're not wanted, that's **officious**. Employees act like that at their offices, being officious to the bosses. So whether low or high tide, Carlito would **abide**, put up with whatever life threw in his eyes. He was **punctilious**, eager to follow the rules, he buttoned every button, always tied his shoes. His number one priority was upholding **propriety**, being polite and maintaining the laws of society.

diminutive (adj.) - miniature, small
goad (v.) - to urge, to provoke into action
lachrymose (adj.) - tearful

obsequious (adj.) - submissive

laud (v.) - to applaud or praise
sycophant (n.) - a self-serving flatterer

officious (adj.) - offering unwanted help or service

abide (v.) - to put up with, tolerate
punctilious (adj.) - eager to follow rules

propriety (n.) - decency, state of being proper

If you don't stand strong you get knocked around, fortify like a fort or else you'll fall down. Eventually every living thing will fall into the sea, how could I let someone else dictate who I'm gonna be?

One day Carlito took his dog for a walk, **ambling** through Central Park in New York. He heard some guy making some **scurrilous**

amble (v.) - to stroll, walk
scurrilous (adj.) - crude, vulgar

remarks, vulgar words and curses, not sounding very smart. The man's face seemed **inimical** from the start, hostile and enemy-like, covered with scars. Now you should never judge a man 'til you've **trekked** a mile in his shoes, but if he doesn't wear shoes, what you gonna do? An evil, **malevolent** old man, wanted to spit words that were vicious, harmful, and **malicious**. The man looked angry enough to punch, he was **truculent**, **pugnacious**, ready to fight, **belligerent**. The man **accosted** Carlito, confronted him verbally. Carlito got cut so bad you'd think he was in surgery. See sticks and stones have never broken his bones, but **invectives** have made him cry. Carlito was feeling all **timorous** and fearful, he tried acting **circumspect**, **prudent**, and careful. He said, "Hola amigo, que hora es?" The stranger said nothing, just punched him in the chest. BOOM! The man was **nefarious**, evil, and villainous, colder than Sagittarius. The man continued with his **petulance**, his rudeness and irritability, saying, "I want your doggie." He wanted to **repudiate** the offer, turn it down, but the man had his fists in Carlito's face now. He **acceded** to the request, Carlito said "yes." "I guess in this case, bro, you know best." Carlito wanted to be obliging and **accommodating**, but in fact the situation was humiliating.

If you don't stand strong you get knocked around, fortify like a fort or else you'll fall down. Eventually every living thing will fall into the sea, how could I let someone else dictate who I'm gonna be?

inimical (adj.) - hostile, threatening

trek (v.) - to walk, travel by foot

malevolent (adj.) - having intent to harm others
malicious (adj.) - malevolent, harmful
truculent (adj.) - eager to fight, violent
pugnacious (adj.) - belligerent
belligerent (adj.) - contentious, ready to fight
accost (v.) - to approach or confront aggressively
invective (n.) - a verbal attack
timorous (adj.) - fearful, timid
circumspect (adj.) - cautious
prudent (adj.) - cautious, careful

nefarious (adj.) - horribly villainous

petulance (n.) - irritability, impoliteness

repudiate (v.) - to reject, turn down
accede (v.) - to agree

accommodating (adj.) - obliging, helpful

Later that day, I bumped into a crying Carlito. I was **poised** on a bench **masticating** on some nachos, chewing, I said, "Yo bro, how you doing?" He tried to play it off like he was only fooling. He offered the **spurious** excuse that he had something in his eye. Never believe a spurious excuse, it's often a lie. He was crying. He tried to **abate** his shame, lessen his pain, telling me without his dog he would be the same. Then he told me the story, how this man had **abased** him, humiliated and disgraced him. **Lacerations** over both his eyes, he had scars, there had been an **altercation**, a physical confrontation. It was up to me to **mediate** the dispute, like Judge Judy but without the lipstick and attitude. I had to be the **arbitrator**, the go-between. We found the man in the park were he had been. I knew the solution, we needed revenge, **restitution**, some payback, **retaliation**, and **retribution**. I said, "I take **umbrage** at that fact that you stole my friend's pet, my heart's filled with anger and resentment." He tried to down play, but I **upbraided** him, I scolded him severely, criticized and **berated** him. I said, "You need to give that dog back right now, plus I want you to **atone** and apologize right now. You're lucky that I'm feeling **benevolent**, nice, and generous, otherwise I might leave you **bereft** of your esophagus, without your throat, without a hope." The man **conceded**, he gave the dog back. That's the end of the story and the track.

poised (adj.) - balanced, readied
masticate (v.) - to chew

spurious (adj.) - false but intended to seem believable or possible

abate (v.) - to lessen, to reduce in severity

abase (v.) - to lower, demean, degrade
laceration (n.) - a cut, a rip
altercation (n.) - an argument, dispute

mediate (v.) - to intervene, to arbitrate, to sort out
arbitrator (n.) - one who settles controversy between two sides
restitution (n.) - compensation, reimbursement
retaliation (n.) - revenge, punishment
retribution (n.) - vengeance, revenge, payback
umbrage (n.) - anger, offense, resentment
upbraid (v.) - to criticize, scold, reproach
berate (v.) - to scold severely
atone (v.) - to apologize, make amends

benevolent (adj.) - kind, good, caring
bereft (adj.) - without, devoid of

concede (v.) - to give in, to accept

Do You Remember?

Synonym Matching: In the space provided, write the letter of the synonym on the right that corresponds to the word on the left.

1. Goad _____   A. Hostile
2. Amble _____   B. Scold
3. Inimical _____   C. Truculent
4. Pugnacious _____   D. Chew
5. Timorous _____   E. Provoke
6. Nefarious _____   F. Evil
7. Masticate _____   G. Kind
8. Altercation _____   H. Confrontation
9. Upbraid _____   I. Stroll
10. Benevolent _____   J. Fearful

Sentence Completions: Each sentence below has one blank, indicating that something has been omitted. Beneath the sentence are five words labeled A through E. Choose the word that, when inserted in the sentence, best fits the meaning of the sentence as a whole.

1. My dog is so well trained, she _____ fetches my slippers every time I whistle.
A) Indignantly
B) Obsequiously
C) Often
D) Aggressively
E) Ostentatiously

2. "Nothing irritates me more in the classroom than a _____," Mrs. Rodriguez exclaimed. "They're always complimenting my hair to get better grades."
A) Sybarite
B) Hedonist
C) Gourmand
D) Sycophant
E) Pedagogue

3. Stacey D. was _____, and never listened to her iPod in study hall because the sign strictly forbade it.
A) Devious
B) Hypocritical
C) Studious
D) Serene
E) Punctilious

4. Some comedians make their living on _____ jokes, but in my opinion, the true comic genius can keep it clean and still get laughs.
A) Maudlin
B) Scurrilous
C) Sanguine
D) Somnolent
E) Erudite

5. Of all of the Batman characters, the _____ Penguin comes to mind as the most haunting.
A) Munificent
B) Benevolent
C) Nefarious
D) Resplendent
E) Affable

6. The ball was going, going, and then, diving into a pine tree at the fence, Sheena came up with it, her arms covered in _____ from the sharp needles.

A) Lacerations
B) Dogma
C) Quagmires
D) Excursions
E) Munitions

7. There seems to be some _____ on Billy's part ever since Zhuyan stole his girlfriend; he scowls at Z. every time he passes him in the hall.

A) Largess
B) Conciliation
C) Hubris
D) Kudos
E) Umbrage

8. My father _____ the dog for stealing a piece of turkey from the table.
A) Lauded
B) Upbraided
C) Abolished
D) Extolled
E) Excommunicated

9. The _____ old magician smiled down at the small boy as he shared the secrets of his best card trick.
A) Benevolent
B) Inimical
C) Repellent
D) Cerebral
E) Fatuous

10. A raid by hungry brown bears on a recent camping trip left me _____ of food.
A) Negligent
B) Critical
C) Skeptical
D) Bereft
E) Tremulous

Reading Comprehension: Read the passage below and answer the questions based on the text.

Damon's string of bad luck seemed to extend indefinitely. He had quit his job at a local coffee shop after his petulant boss accosted him one day for not being obsequious enough to the customers. Damon had been polite, just not overly sycophantic. Since his boss was also his landlord, Damon should have been prudent and acted circumspectly, but he was angry that his boss had abased him in front of other employees. Damon berated his boss, yelling that he was a malicious, malevolent, nefarious old man. When his landlord-boss told him that he had better move out of the apartment, Damon found himself simultaneously bereft of his job and his place to live.

1. As used in the passage above, the word "prudent" is a(n):
(A) Adjective
(B) Adverb
(C) Noun
(D) Verb
(E) Preposition

2. The reason that Damon's boss yelled at him at work is that:
(A) Damon was always angry.
(B) He thought that Damon was overly malicious.
(C) Damon wasn't officious enough to the customers.
(D) Damon had abased him in front of the employees.
(E) He was Damon's landlord.

Phobia

Word Bank

Daunting
Feral
Abhor
Destitute
Abject
Domicile
Derelict
Defunct
Requisition
Renovate
Affluent
Raze
Reprehensible
Dilapidated
Exacerbate
Pacify
Allay
Assuage
Anxiety
Sedate
Sobriety
Agoraphobia

Claustrophobia
Diaphanous
Harrowing
Strenuous
Canvas
Ascetic
Quaint
Reel
Redoubtable
Formidable
Austere
Taciturn
Enervate
Abscond
Desolate
Despondent
Forlorn

These some haunting raps, what you think about that? Might be a **daunting** task, but we on through that. I'm seeing nine black cats with some teeth to match, savage beasts wearing **feral** masks.

There is this house I **abhor** and hate, it's all dark on the corner of my block. I live among the impoverished and **destitute**, the **abject** poor, here's the proof: the **domicile** was **derelict**, all run-down, no sun now, we call the block mud town. It was a **defunct** warehouse, no longer used, the kids used to throw bottles at the windows after school. The government demanded the house made a **requisition**, they wanted to **renovate** it, fix it up for the rich and the **affluent**, those who have money, it's crummy some wanted to knock it down, **raze** the house. Damn! So damn cruel and **reprehensible** the way the politicians treat the poor like they're dispensable. The house stayed put, remained **dilapidated**, in a state of disrepair so the neighbors hate it. My fear was **exacerbated** by this fact, made more intense by this fact. My friends tried to **pacify** me, **allay** my fears, stop my tears, **assuage** my fears, soothe me like Jimmy Page drinking a smoothie, before a show to calm his **anxiety**, **sedate** himself into a state of **sobriety**. Hip-hop heads screaming, "Who's he?" He's the ghost in these . . .

Haunting raps . . .

I'm **agoraphobic**: scared of open spaces, **claustrophobic**: scared of confined spaces, so I'm doubly screwed, know what I mean dude? At least I'm transparent like

daunting (adj.) - intimidating

feral (adj.) - savage, wild, untamed

abhor (v.) - to hate, loathe

destitute (adj.) - impoverished
abject (adj.) - of the most miserable or contemptible kind
domicile (n.) - a residence, a home
derelict (adj.) - run-down, abandoned
defunct (adj.) - no longer used or existing
requisition (n.) - a demand for goods, often by an authority
renovate (v.) - to restore, return to original state
affluent (adj.) - rich, wealthy
raze (v.) - to demolish
reprehensible (adj.) - deserving of criticism

dilapidated (adj.) - in a state of disrepair

exacerbate (v.) - to make more violent, intense
pacify (v.) - to sooth, ease
allay (v.) - to soothe, assuage
assuage (v.) - to ease, pacify
anxiety (n.) - uneasiness
sedate (v.) - to calm, soothe
sobriety (n.) - moderation from excess, or calm tranquility

agoraphobia (n.) - an abnormal fear of open or public places
claustrophobia (n.) - an abnormal fear of closed or crowded spaces

diaphanous screens letting light through. I live in fear, it sounds queer, I have **harrowing** experiences year after year. Just to step out my door is a **strenuous** task, requiring strength like a **canvas** needs paint, an **ascetic** practices restraint, he ain't eating caviar, he's sitting in his old house it's kind of **quaint**, but not this frickin' haunted house, it's all that I'm seeing, up to the ceiling, spider webs leaving me **reeling**. Against the stormy day this house is **redoubtable**, arouses dread and alarm, it's **formidable**. The **austere** appearance, bare, and bleak, makes me **taciturn**, I'm too scared to speak. This experience **enervates** me, I need sleep. I need to **abscond**, hide out, and I'm gonna sneak. The **desolate**, deserted, dreary landscape, makes me wish I was at home eating my mama's pancakes. I'm feeling **despondent**, distressed, and hopeless, I'm not the dopest maybe I'm just a dope, I'm **forlorn**, I'm lonely, I have no hope,

Haunting raps . . .

diaphanous (adj.) - transparent, light, airy
harrowing (adj.) - agonizing, distressing
strenuous (adj.) - requiring tremendous strength or energy
canvas (n.) - a piece of cloth on which an artist paints
ascetic (n.) - one who practices restraint as a means of self-discipline, usually religious
quaint (adj.) - old-fashioned
reel (v.) - to be thrown off balance or feel dizzy
redoubtable (adj.) - formidable, commanding respect
formidable (adj.) - arousing fear or alarm
austere (adj.) - very bare, bleak, simple
taciturn (adj.) - not inclined to talk
enervate (v.) - to weaken, make weary
abscond (v.) - to sneak away and hide
desolate (adj.) - deserted, lifeless
despondent (adj.) - discouraged, hopeless, depressed
forlorn (adj.) - lonely, hopeless

Do You Remember?

Synonym Matching: In the space provided, write the letter of the synonym on the right that corresponds to the word on the left.

1. Domicile ____
2. Abhor ____
3. Pacify ____
4. Harrowing ____
5. Austere ____
6. Forlorn ____
7. Abscond ____
8. Redoubtable ____
9. Sedate ____
10. Anxiety ____

A. Tranquilize
B. Uneasiness
C. Frightful
D. Hopeless
E. Agonizing
F. Soothe
G. House
H. Hate
I. Sneak
J. Simple

Sentence Completions: Each sentence below has one blank, indicating that something has been omitted. Beneath the sentence are five words labeled A through E. Choose the word that, when inserted in the sentence, best fits the meaning of the sentence as a whole.

1. That cat looks much too _____ to be a house cat; it must have been raised in the wild.
A) Charming
B) Grandiose
C) Obtuse
D) Feral
E) Delicate

2. News of yet another kidnapping _____ Jane's fear of strangers.
A) Assuaged
B) Belittled
C) Alleviated
D) Elucidated
E) Exacerbated

3. As head of the Pacification Department, Lauren's job was to promote _____ among the populace during times of potential panic.
A) Mutability
B) Anarchy
C) Apathy
D) Sobriety
E) Propriety

4. Quentin was never very good at indoor hide-and-seek, mainly because his _____ prevented him from hiding in the closets.
A) Agoraphobia
B) Sensitivity
C) Claustrophobia
D) Gaudiness
E) Emaciation

5. Wen bought some _____ curtains to allow some sunlight into his room, while still maintaining his privacy.
A) Opaque
B) Fetid
C) Diaphanous
D) Lucid
E) Ethereal

6. Though Siddhartha came from a wealthy family, he ended up living the life of a(n) _____, devoid of luxury.
A) Voluptuary
B) Ascetic
C) Anarchist
D) Pacifist
E) Hedonist

7. Grandma had lots of old-fashioned things in her house, but of all her ancient knick-knacks, I always found her cuckoo clock to be the most _____.
A) Vulgar
B) Stoic
C) Quaint
D) Ostentatious
E) Statuesque

8. Watching him prance nimbly in the ring before the fight, Foreman had to admit that Ali was a truly _____ opponent.
A) Formidable
B) Callous
C) Profane
D) Languid
E) Effete

9. Shopping _____ me so much that I often fall asleep on the bus ride home from the mall.
A) Invigorates
B) Enervates
C) Extricate
D) Satiates
E) Placate

10. Some enthusiasts who dreamed of life on Mars were upset by the pictures that showed the planet's rocky, _____ landscape.
A) Vibrant
B) Dynamic
C) Desolate
D) Iridescent
E) Diaphanous

Reading Comprehension: Read the passage below and answer the questions based on the text.

I have to be honest: I don't like my mother-in-law very much. It's not that I abhor her or anything, it's just that she's so anxious all the time, it's a little hard to deal with. It's always a daunting task whenever she comes over to dinner. No matter what I cook, we have to allay all of her fears about the food before she'll take a single bite. And it's pretty hard to pacify her once she gets excited. One time, when I cooked rabbit stew, she got so worked up that she told me that cooking rabbit was reprehensible, that you should only cook feral animals. I asked her if she considered a cow to be a feral animal, but she wouldn't answer me. Instead she ate nothing and remained taciturn for the rest of the dinner. Her visits are so exhausting and enervating!

1. The tone in the passage is best described as:
(A) Analytical
(B) Skeptical
(C) Reverent
(D) Hateful
(E) Annoyed

2. The word "allay" in the passage above most closely means:
(A) Cook
(B) Assuage
(C) Discuss
(D) Exemplify
(E) Answer

Friends

Word Bank

Gilded	Jubilant	Impudent
Concoct	Alleviate	Puerile
Indignation	Chastise	Juvenile
Patent	Elucidate	Guile
Inextricable	Limpid	Bilk
Discreet	Ultimate	Telepathic
Surreptitious	Choreographed	Soothsayer
Alacrity	Idolatrous	Seer
Manifest	Fawn	Inveterate
Erect	Extol	Delude
Grandiose	Diaphanous	Compel
Meager	Spectral	Camaraderie
Envious	Apparitional	
Magnanimous	Lethargic	
Munificent	Comatose	
Affable	Benign	
Amiable	Mendacious	
Conciliatory	Calumny	
Hierarchy	Defame	
Linchpin	Libel	
Weather	Slander	
Inclement	Malign	

Made new friends, but I kept the old ones, some are **gilded** and some are golden, made new friends, but I kept the old ones.

Sometimes I think about the time when I was five years old, on the jungle gym climbing. I'm not **concocting** this story, not making it up, I had torn my britches, you could see my booty. I frowned with **indignation**, 'cause it wasn't fair, my situation was **patently**, clearly unfair. I thought it was an **inextricable** situation, with no way out like a hedge maze when my friend Brendan came over to me, and told me how to walk out of there **discreetly**, **surreptitiously**, so that no one could see me. We moved with **alacrity** and quickly. Our friendship next **manifested** and showed itself at his house, **erecting** pillow-forts on his couch. He built a **grandiose** fort with a tower in back. My fort was so **meager** it looked like a shack. I was feeling jealous and **envious**. He was **magnanimous** enough, generous enough, **munificent** enough to let me come into his fort and play with his stuff. Now that's a true friend . . .

Made new friends, but I kept the old ones, some are gilded and some are golden, made new friends, but I kept the old ones.

Now a girlfriend can be your best friend, too, you can play chess and you can practice jujitsu. My girl's so **affable** and **amiable**, she's always acting **conciliatory** and agreeable. You know there's no **hierarchy** in our relationship, we're on the same plane like Wes Snipes and terrorists. Like the **linchpin** in my life, you know she holds everything

gilded (adj.) - covered with a thin layer of gold, or deceptively attractive

concoct (v.) - to make up or invent
indignation (n.) - anger due to an unfair situation
patent (adj.) - clear, apparent
inextricable (adj.) - hopelessly confused or tangled

discreet (adj.) - prudent or inconspicuous
surreptitious (adj.) - done in a secret or stealthy way
alacrity (n.) - speed, readiness
manifest (v.) - to show clearly
erect (v.) - to construct, to raise
grandiose (adj.) - extraordinary, grand in scope
meager (adj.) - lacking in quality or stature
envious (adj.) - jealous
magnanimous (adj.) - generous, noble
munificent (adj.) - generous, benevolent

affable (adj.) - friendly, amiable
amiable (adj.) - friendly, affable
conciliatory (adj.) - agreeable, friendly
hierarchy (n.) - a ranking system of groups or individuals
linchpin (n.) - something that holds separate things together
weather (v.) - to withstand or survive a situation
inclement (adj.) - stormy, bad, severe
jubilant (adj.) - joyful, happy

together, so when we **weather** the storm, and whether the weather is **inclement** or sunny, we carry on like that bunny with the drum, joyful, **jubilant**, always having fun. When I'm feeling blue, she **alleviates** my symptoms like a drug. If I'm acting like a thug she's going to **chastise** me, criticize me severely, **elucidates** my problems, clarifies them clearly. We keep communication **limpid**, not too complex, clearer than a window that just got Windexed. We'll be together to the **ultimate**, together to the last, the way we dance like we've just been **choreographed**. I don't mean to be **idolatrous**, **fawn** over her too much, but I need to **extol** and praise her.

Made new friends, but I kept the old ones, some are gilded and some are golden, made new friends, but I kept the old ones.

Your friends might be less visible, too, I have a **diaphanous** friend who's completely see-through. He's **spectral** and **apparitional** like a ghost, not in a coma but so **lethargic**, he's **comatose**. Like a tiger full of tranquilizers, he's mostly **benign**, but sometimes he gets **mendacious** and then he starts lying. He attempts **calumny**, tries to **defame** people spreading lies, **libel**, and **slander**, he **maligns** them forever. An **impudent** and rude guy, he's **puerile**, **juvenile**, immature, he's full of **guile**, deceitful, he **bilks** me out of milk money, cheats me, beats me at Guess Who?, he guesses correctly. He's **telepathic**, a mind reader, a **soothsayer**, fortune-teller, a **seer**. He's an **inveterate** prankster, who pulled pranks since he was born, he'll star-sixty-nine my friends when I get off the phone. He'll

alleviate (v.) - to relieve

chastise (v.) - to criticize, to scold

elucidate (v.) - to clarify

limpid (adj.) - clear, easily understood

ultimate (n.) - the last part, or a fundamental element

choreographed (adj.) - arranged, as in dance

idolatrous (adj.) - worshiping excessively an object or person

fawn (v.) - to show affection through flattery

extol (v.) - to praise highly

diaphanous (adj.) - transparent, see-through

spectral (adj.) - ghostly

apparitional (adj.) - ghostly, spectral

lethargic (adj.) - lazy, apathetic

comatose (adj.) - lethargic

benign (adj.) - nonthreatening, innocuous

mendacious (adj.) - inclined to lie or mislead

calumny (n.) - an attempt to defame another's reputation

defame (v.) - to destroy the reputation of

libel (n.) - a statement that gives an unjust or unfavorable representation of a person or thing, a defamation

slander (n.) - a false statement to damage the reputation of another

malign (v.) - to slander, to smear, to libel, to defame, to speak evil of

impudent (adj.) - rude, improper

puerile (adj.) - immature

juvenile (adj.) - young or immature

guile (n.) - deceitful actions or behavior

bilk (v.) - to cheat, to swindle

telepathic (adj.) - capable of reading minds

soothsayer (n.) - a fortune teller

seer (n.) - a fortune teller

inveterate (adj.) - habitual, natural

delude my friends into believing he's me, we have the same voice, they have no choice, they're **compelled** to believe. Despite that we're good friends, live in **camaraderie**, share our desserts, we share a brain, he's a part of me . . .

Made new friends, but I kept the old ones, some are gilded and some are golden, made new friends, but I kept the old ones.

delude (v.) - to deceive, to mislead
compel (v.) - to force
camaraderie (n.) - cheerful unity among a group

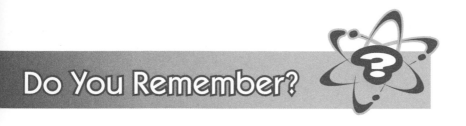

Synonym Matching: In the space provided, write the letter of the synonym on the right that corresponds to the word on the left.

1. Discreet _____
2. Manifest _____
3. Magnanimous _____
4. Affable _____
5. Jubilant _____
6. Elucidate _____
7. Extol _____
8. Diaphanous _____
9. Puerile _____
10. Camaraderie _____

A. Amiable
B. Clarify
C. Praise
D. Joyful
E. Show
F. Transparent
G. Juvenile
H. Friendship
I. Prudent
J. Munificent

Sentence Completions: Each sentence below has one blank, indicating that something has been omitted. Beneath the sentence are five words labeled A through E. Choose the word that, when inserted in the sentence, best fits the meaning of the sentence as a whole.

1. Though she did not hand in the homework assignment, you must give Yee-chin some credit for _____ such a fantastic excuse.

A) Delineating
B) Extrapolating
C) Concocting
D) Introducing
E) Abrogating

2. Philo had planned on firing Alvaro on account of his laziness, but he soon began mopping with such consistent _____ that she had no choice but to keep him on staff.
A) Bluster
B) Resiliency
C) Ennui
D) Fortification
E) Alacrity

3. The whole class was _____ of Joe when he rolled up to school on Monday; that new Escalade was hot!
A) Tired
B) Critical
C) Judgmental
D) Envious
E) Possessive

4. Dave Matthews is one of the most _____ rock stars; I heard he gave more than a million dollars to charity in 2004.
A) Irascible
B) Munificent
C) Benevolent
D) Stingy
E) Frugal

5. The rice-throwing crowd was _____ as the gleaming bride and groom strolled down the stairs.
A) Sober
B) Jubilant
C) Indignant
D) Sedated
E) Belligerent

6. Parker was severely _____ for carving his name in the school desk.
A) Chastised
B) Lauded
C) Commended
D) Repudiated
E) Slandered

7. Jethro was a(n) _____ Red Sox fan, and really annoyed his friends by constantly talking about how he and Johnny Damon were "pretty much the same person."
A) Oblivious
B) Obvious
C) Magnanimous
D) Licentious
E) Idolatrous

8. Sometimes when it rains, I get so _____ that I can't seem to do anything but watch Gilligan's Island marathons on TV Land.
A) Lethargic
B) Invigorated
C) Satiated
D) Saturated
E) Irascible

9. I get so sick of those TV psychics who claim that they're _____.
A) Sympathetic
B) Emphatic
C) Telepathic
D) Telegraphic
E) Ingenious

10. Though incredulous at first, after Rosalio showed us his authentic moon rock, we were _____ to believe that he had actually visited the moon.
A) Reluctant
B) Eager
C) Happy
D) Predisposed
E) Compelled

Reading Comprehension: Read the passage below and answer the questions based on the text.

The royal palace is a building with such ornate architecture that it inspires idolatrous praise in all those who gaze upon it. A pride of benign lions lounges comatosely on the front steps, unless the weather is inclement, in which case they are brought inside. If you step through the grandiose doors, you are immediately greeted by an affable old butler who leads you discreetly past the rows of armed guards. In the royal hall, troops of jubilant dancers prance about in perfect choreography before the king. Next to the king is the ever-present seer, whose prophecies alleviate the anxieties of the nervous king as a lullaby might calm a baby. Whether the soothsayer is mendacious and just concocts his predictions or whether he has legitimate telepathic abilities remains a point of dispute in the royal court.

1. The phrase "as a lullaby might calm a baby" is an example of:
(A) Metaphor
(B) Simile
(C) Personification
(D) Allusion
(E) Irony

2. According to the author, the thing that is most awe-inspiring about the palace for visitors is:
(A) The royal soothsayer
(B) The friendly butler
(C) The grandiose doors
(D) The ornate architecture
(E) The pride of lions

Flo + Cab

Word Bank

Collusion
Exigent
Confluence
Discrete
Divergent
Divisive
Disparage
Impervious
Coalesce
Apocalypse
Juxtapose
Variegate
Differentiate
Ameliorate
Oration
Accentuate
Sanguine
Enervated
Saccharine
Maudlin
Mores
Cavity

Amalgamation
Copious
Connotation
Diverse
Terse
Preponderance
Dissonance
Cacophony
Harmony
Concord
Confound
Scourge
Scathing
Indictment
Retract

Like a boomerang we're back, together
again, the **collusion**, two people huddled
and making a plan.Rocking iPods to Etch-A-
Sketches, it's Escher, urgent and **exigent**,
exerting mad pressure. Like how peanut butter
always tastes better with jelly, we added
flow to vocab, to get Flocabulary. It's the
confluence of two **discrete** things, like french
fries and onion rings, we make things meet
that are different. Now sometimes it's true that
divergent things, split people apart and are
divisive. Some people try to **disparage**
our project, speak ill of it and criticize us,
but we're **impervious** to bad vibes, we're
untouchable, stick together like Heathcliff and
Claire Huxtable. Two things come together just
coalesce like when you zip up the
two sides of your vest.

F L O   C A B
wherever you go we'll be there.
F L O   C A B
rocking harder than your grandma's chair.
F L O C A B
rocking the **apocalypse** until there's nothing
left.
F L O C A B
a better recipe for success than the Iron Chef.

We **juxtapose** those who know and those
who don't, by putting them together to
compare and contrast. We **variegate** and
differentiate these tracks, so they don't all
run together like sidewalk chalk in the rain.
We **ameliorate** our **orations**, make our
speeches better, improve and troubleshoot,
don't maintain. I stress and **accentuate**
positivity in life, like peas accentuate the taste

collusion (n.) - a conspiracy, a secret
agreement
exigent (adj.) - critical, urgent

confluence (n.) - a convergence, a coming
together
discrete (adj.) - separate, distinct, individual
divergent (adj.) - different, deviating, contrary
divisive (adj.) - causing conflict, opposition
disparage (v.) - to criticize, degrade, belittle
impervious (adj.) - unable to be penetrated,
unaffected

coalesce (v.) - to combine into one

apocalypse (n.) - total devastation, the end of
the world

juxtapose (v.) - to put next to each other

variegate (v.) - to diversify
differentiate (v.) - to distinguish, to make
different
ameliorate (v.) - to improve, to make better
oration (n.) - a dignified and formal speech
accentuate (v.) - to emphasize, to highlight

of rice. So I'm **sanguine**, optimistic, and cheery, the opposite of **enervated** and weary, you hear me, clearly, we spread good vibes like Beverly Cleary, but not as **saccharine**, overly sweet. **Maudlin** is sentimental like your dentals are your teeth. We fight holes in our **mores**, those moral **cavities**. The **amalgamation**, combination of two rare things, I can't believe it's so butter . . .

sanguine (adj.) - cheery, optimistic, hopeful
enervated (adj.) - lacking energy, weakened, exhausted
saccharine (adj.) - overly sweet
maudlin (adj.) - sentimental
mores (n.) - moral attitudes
cavity (n.) - a hole
amalgamation (n.) - a union, a merger

F L O C A B
wherever you go we'll be there.
F L O C A B
rocking harder than your grandma's chair.
Γ L O C A B
rocking the apocalypse until there's nothing left.
F L O C A B
a better recipe for success than the Iron Chef.

There are **copious connotations** for every single word, many meanings that are varied and **diverse**. So I could be **terse**, and not talk with too many words, and a **preponderance** of meanings could still emerge. Some say different voices create **dissonance**, white noise, and **cacophony**, actually they make harmony. And without **harmony**, BoyzIIMen would still be boys, and Art Garfunkel would have been unemployed. We're in harmonious agreement, in **concord**, like the fast plane and we'd like you to get on board. We **confound** and frustrate those who must hate us, and think hip-hop is the **scourge** of the English language. They offer **scathing** criticism and **indictments**. They think that when you're studying there should be no excitement, but then they listen to our songs, they **retract** and withdraw their statements like it was a bank card.

copious (adj.) - abundant, plentiful
connotation (n.) - a meaning or association suggested by a word beyond its definition
diverse (adj.) - varied
terse (adj.) - abrupt, short, brief
preponderance (n.) - a great amount or frequency
dissonance (n.) - lack of harmony or agreement
cacophony (n.) - noise, discordant sound
harmony (n.) - agreement, often of sound
concord (n.) - agreement
confound (v.) - to frustrate
scourge (n.) - a plague
scathing (adj.) - hurtful, critical
indictment (n.) - accusation of wrongdoing

retract (v.) – withdraw

FLOCAB

wherever you go we'll be there.

FLOCAB

rocking harder than your grandma's chair.

FLOCAB

rocking the apocalypse until there's nothing left.

FLOCAB

a better recipe for success than the Iron Chef

Do You Remember?

Synonym Matching: In the space provided, write the letter of the synonym on the right that corresponds to the word on the left.

1. Exigent _____   A. Sentimental
2. Sanguine _____   B. Improve
3. Saccharine _____   C. Succinct
4. Maudlin _____   D. Urgent
5. Concord _____   E. Frustrate
6. Ameliorate _____   F. Optimistic
7. Terse _____   G. Withdraw
8. Amalgamate _____   H. Sweet
9. Confound _____   I. Agreement
10. Retract _____   J. Combine

Sentence Completions: Each sentence below has one blank, indicating that something has been omitted. Beneath the sentence are five words labeled A through E. Choose the word that, when inserted in the sentence, best fits the meaning of the sentence as a whole.

1. Many say that Yoko Ono was a _____ force between John Lennon and the rest of The Beatles, and that she may be responsible for the band's demise.
A) Creative
B) Conciliatory
C) Divisive
D) Decisive
E) Reputable

2. When I bought my winter coat, the zealous salesman carried on about how it was _____ to both wind and cold.
A) Vulnerable
B) Susceptible
C) Adherent
D) Imperious
E) Impervious

3. The Peterson Triplets always dressed the same and were nearly impossible to
____.
A) Repudiate
B) Differentiate
C) Obfuscate
D) Clarify
E) Aggregate

4. Tiffany's engagement ring was a hideous _____ of gold and turquoise.
A) Amalgamation
B) Umbrage
C) Amenity
D) Discrepancy
E) Convention

5. Rodrigo was a fantastic student and made sure to take _____ notes in every
class.
A) Shoddy
B) Dubious
C) Inimical
D) Copious
E) Disheartened

6. Dr. Bandahar was a man of few words and was known for his _____
replies in press conferences.
A) Verbose
B) Loquacious
C) Sagacious
D) Terse
E) Tenuous

7. When the goose ran out of the pen, there arose such a clamor; the dogs
howled and barked in utter _____.
A) Tranquility
B) Cacophony
C) Harmony
D) Turpitude
E) Grandiloquence

8. When asked what she would do with the one billion dollars, the Miss America contestant said that she would try to bring about communication and _____ between all warring nations.
A) Enmity
B) Tenacity
C) Pulchritude
D) Belligerence
E) Harmony

9. I'll never forget the _____ words Rafael used when he viciously accused Sophia of cheating on him.
A) Scathing
B) Laudatory
C) Scintillating
D) Circumspect
E) Saccharine

10. The CEO was served with several _____ based on his involvement with insider trading and embezzlement.
A) Quandaries
B) Indictments
C) Paradoxes
D) Quagmires
E) Tributes

Reading Comprehension: Read the passage below and answer the questions based on the text.

A few years ago, a major tobacco company came out with a controversial new product called Baby-Smokes. Confounded by the huge number of nonsmokers in the baby community, the company developed this novel amalgamation as a way of ameliorating their revenue. The company argued that, while typically thought of as divergent things occupying two very discrete spaces in our culture and society, babies and smoking were in fact a perfect combination. Babies, the company said, loved having things in their mouths. Why not a cigarette? Obviously this product inspired a huge amount of scathing criticism from the general public, who found that Baby-Smokes offended their very mores. The product was quickly recalled.

1. The main reason that the tobacco company developed Baby-Smokes was:
(A) Any press is good press.
(B) They wanted to do something novel.
(C) They wanted to make more money.
(D) They thought babies would like cigarettes.
(E) Babies and smoking were a perfect combination.

2. The word "mores" in the passage above most closely means:
(A) Paradigms
(B) Ideas
(C) Souls
(D) Communities
(E) Values

Myriad Operations

Word Bank

Espy	Refrain	Aloof
Uncanny	Foster	Bard
Hail	Supplant	Travesty
Terrestrial	Whet	Tragedy
Celestial	Akimbo	Parody
Winsome	Swarthy	Anomaly
Presumptuous	Ruddy	Ubiquitous
Brash	Exorbitant	Obsequious
Brazen	Veneer	Submissive
Audacious	Complicit	
Brusque	Obdurate	
Incisive	Cajole	
Succinct	Aggrandize	
Cursory	Pulchritude	
Contusion	Torrid	
Laceration	Sate	
Acute	Satiate	
Callous	Abort	
Credulity	Battery	
Myriad	Compliment	
Pertinacious	Ethereal	
Metamorphosis	Sagacious	

I was at the Taqueria thinking taco or enchilada, when I **espied** this smart and pretty Latin mama. This girl was so beautiful it was supernatural and **uncanny**, I think she **hailed** from um, Miami. I told her I come from deep within the Earth, I'm **terrestrial**, compared to me, you're from the sky, you're **celestial**. You're **winsome**. I mean you win some and you lose some, but girl you're winsome, I mean very attractive. She scolded me told me I was overly bold and **presumptuous**, too **brash**, too **brazen**, too **audacious**. Her manner was **brusque**, her speech short and abrupt, with these two little letters she said, "loco give it up." (No!) Let me be **incisive**, clear sharp and direct. Let me be **succinct**, just as brief as I can get. She shot me with a quick, **cursory** glance, hit like a dagger, caused a **contusion**, started bruising, and then I staggered. She scarred me, gave me a **laceration** over my heart piece, the pain was **acute**, sharper than a set of sharp teeth, but even though she acted so **callous** and cold, I had no **credulity**, I couldn't believe what I was being told.

She said "no."
I said you don't know so,
there are **myriad** operations I could undergo.

I don't mean to be **pertinacious** as in stubbornly persistent. I would operate on myself, girl, if you was my assistant, I would undergo a total **metamorphosis**, and more than this, I would **refrain** from eating all them bacon bits and sausages. To **foster** good health and promote good health within myself, I would **supplant** my supply of whole milk with skim milk on my shelf. You **whet** my appetite,

espy (v.) - to catch sight of, glimpse

uncanny (adj.) - of supernatural character or origin

hail (v.) - to come from

terrestrial (adj.) - relating to the land

celestial (adj.) - relating to the sky or the heavens

winsome (adj.) - charming, attractive

presumptuous (adj.) - disrespectfully bold

brash (adj.) - hasty or lacking in sensitivity

brazen (adj.) - excessively bold, brash

audacious (adj.) - excessively bold

brusque (adj.) - short, abrupt, dismissive

incisive (adj.) - clear, sharp, direct

succinct (adj.) - marked by compact precision

cursory (adj.) - brief to the point of being superficial

contusion (n.) - bruise, injury

laceration (n.) - a cut, tear

acute (adj.) - sharp, severe

callous (adj.) - harsh, cold, unfeeling

credulity (n.) - readiness to believe

myriad (adj.) - consisting of a very great number

pertinacious (adj.) - stubbornly persistent, holding to a belief or position

metamorphosis (n.) - a change of form, shape, substance

refrain (v.) - to hold oneself back, forbear

foster (v.) - to stimulate, promote, encourage

supplant (v.) - to displace and substitute for another

whet (v.) - to make more keen, stimulate

is yours whet back? It's 'round midnight, how 'bout a late night snack? Oh, I sounded like a bimbo, a salesman who couldn't sell though. She stood arms **akimbo**, bent at the elbow. My skin was more **swarthy** and **ruddy** than the fur of Elmo, dark and red, I was blushing **exorbitantly**, excessively. I tried to smile to keep up the **veneer** of respectability, but my tongue was **complicit** in my mind's crimes like an accessory to murder, and I was killing any chance of a first date. She didn't yield to my persuasions, she was **obdurate**. It's pathetic how I tried to get a date by **cajoling** and coaxing, **aggrandizing** my traits, exaggerating and boasting. She said, "Oh no you didn't," like she had an attitude. I was staring at her physical beauty, her **pulchritude**.

She said "no" . . .

This is not a love song, 'cause no love was created, dreamt of a **torrid** hot love, but it wasn't fated. I thought she was hungry for love, she was **sated** and **satiated**, no appetite so I had to **abort** the effort so I gave it up, and tried to launch a **battery** of flattery at her, an assault of **compliments**, it made no dent on her presence. So heavenly, she was **ethereal**, delicate, and refined, I knew I'd never, ever find someone of her kind. She was wise and **sagacious** like a wisdom tooth, while I tried to get in closer she remained **aloof**. I tried to spit some poetry like a poet or a **bard**, but it came out kind of corny, spitting poetry is hard. It was a **travesty**, now kids don't think that a travesty's the same thing as a **tragedy**, 'cause a tragedy is the opposite of a comedy.

akimbo (adj.) - with hands on hips and elbows extending outward

swarthy (adj.) - of dark color or complexion

ruddy (adj.) - having a healthy, reddish color

exorbitant (adj.) - excessive

veneer (n.) - a superficial or deceptively attractive appearance, façade

complicit (adj.) - being an accomplice in a wrongful act

obdurate (adj.) - unyielding to persuasion or moral influences

cajole (v.) - to urge, coax

aggrandize (v.) - to increase or make greater

pulchritude (n.) - physical beauty

torrid (adj.) - giving off intense heat, passionate

sate (v.) - to satisfy (an appetite) fully

satiate (v.) - to satisfy excessively

abort (v.) - to give up on a half-finished project or effort

battery (n.) - an assault or an array of similar things intended for use together

compliment (n.) - an expression of esteem or approval

ethereal (adj.) - heavenly, exceptionally delicate or refined

sagacious (adj.) - shrewd, showing sound judgment

aloof (adj.) - reserved, distant

bard (n.) - a poet, often a singer as well

travesty (n.) - a grossly inferior imitation

tragedy (n.) - a disastrous event, or a work of art in which the hero meets a terrible fate

A travesty is a bad imitation or a **parody**. I'd like to say the interaction was weird like an **anomaly**, but honestly this stuff happens quite often to me, and shorteez frowning at me appear **ubiquitously**, they're everywhere in the world like American currency, I bow down to them **obsequiously** and **submissively**.

She said "no" . . .

parody (n.) - a satirical imitation

anomaly (n.) - something that does not fit into the normal order

ubiquitous (adj.) - existing everywhere, widespread

obsequious (adj.) - excessively compliant or submissive

submissive (adj.) - easily yielding to authority

Synonym Matching: In the space provided, write the letter of the synonym on the right that corresponds to the word on the left.

1. Uncanny _____
2. Winsome _____
3. Incisive _____
4. Acute _____
5. Cajole _____
6. Pulchritude _____
7. Aloof _____
8. Obsequious _____
9. Parody _____
10. Foster _____

A. Coax
B. Severe
C. Beauty
D. Attractive
E. Reserved
F. Supernatural
G. Direct
H. Encourage
I. Submissive
J. Satire

Sentence Completions: Each sentence below has one blank, indicating that something has been omitted. Beneath the sentence are five words labeled A through E. Choose the word that, when inserted in the sentence, best fits the meaning of the sentence as a whole.

1. Comets and stars are _____ bodies.
A) Abnormal
B) Celestial
C) Static
D) Terrestrial
E) Orbital

2. The tightrope walker planned a(n) _____ feat: to walk on a rope from Paris to London.
A) Feeble
B) Facile
C) Ribald
D) Despondent
E) Audacious

3. When Allison fell off her bike it left several blue _____ up and down her leg.
A) Kudos
B) Infamy
C) Lacerations
D) Contusions
E) Panacea

4. Finally Tim gave in to his sister's _____ insistence that he name his pet lobster,
"the Fobster."
A) Flaccid
B) Cogent
C) Pertinacious
D) Dour
E) Callous

5. Not only was the young man late for work, but during the night he had undergone a _____ from a human to a cockroach.
A) Denigration
B) Immersion
C) Transportation
D) Transposition
E) Metamorphosis

6. He was a dark-skinned pirate and had a tendency to wave a fan in front of his _____face.
A) Swarthy
B) Supple
C) Equine
D) Pallid
E) Sordid

7. The _____old woman refused to pay the milkman, swearing she hadn't had a glass of milk in over a decade.
A) Munificent
B) Insightful
C) Opulent
D) Obdurate
E) Magnanimous

8. When it came to electing a Corn Growers Association president, everyone turned to the most _____ member: old Jim "Corn Eyes."
A) Inarticulate
B) Obdurate
C) Aloof
D) Brash
E) Sagacious

9. She was a feisty _____, wandering from village to village composing little tunes about acorns, squash, and the coming apocalypse.
A) Insurgent
B) Maelstrom
C) Bard
D) Antagonist
E) Deacon

10. Leena disliked Lauren Hill's singing voice and thought that her version of "Killing Me Softly" was a complete _____ of the original.
A) Tragedy
B) Travesly
C) Imitation
D) Duplicate
E) Manifestation

Reading Comprehension: Read the passage below and answer the questions based on the text.

One day, when Juana was walking down the street, she espied a man holding a delicious looking burrito, the sight of which whet her appetite to such an extent that she decided to hop into a nearby taqueria and see if she couldn't sate her growing hunger. The exorbitant prices on the menu inside (six dollars for a taco) made the restaurant a true anomaly in the typically cheap neighborhood. Juana, who usually refrained from spending too much money on food, considered aborting her taco-run, but then reconsidered when she caught sight of the myriad fresh salsas they had lined up on a table. Juana ordered a chicken super-burrito and asked the clerk, "I don't mean to be too presumptuous, but could you please supplant the cheese with extra sour cream?" The clerk, who bore an uncanny resemblance to Christopher Walken, nodded brusquely in response.

1. The tone that Juana uses with the clerk in the taqueria is one of:
(A) Flippancy
(B) Politeness
(C) Annoyance
(D) Brashness
(E) Bashfulness

2. The restaurant was relatively unique in the neighborhood because:
(A) They served tacos and burritos.
(B) They had bad service.
(C) They had a large selection of salsas.
(D) They could easily make substitutions.
(E) They had high prices.

I Do

Word Bank

Infuse	Maxim	Bourgeois
Quid Pro Quo	Dutiful	Lavish
Gluttonous	Captivate	Buffet
Portly	Abduct	Bloated
Surfeit	Henchman	Lethargic
Gourmand	Stagnate	Corpulent
Noisome	Stagnant	
Noxious	Torpid	
Baleful	Doppelganger	
Odious	Mimic	
Toothsome	Excursion	
Pungent	Tortuous	
Putrid	Surmise	
Rancid	Espouse	
Forsake	Matrimony	
Somnolent	Laudatory	
Vivacious	Euphoric	
Abbreviate	Gay	
Aphorism	Ruse	
Abridge	Cavort	
Pellucid	Carouse	
Acumen	Buffet	

We inject and **infuse** vocab into raps, raps into the classroom, it's 2 class acts. If I give something to you and get something else back, that's a **quid pro quo**, like we scratch each others' backs. To a gluttonous man, a hamburger is a snack. Often **gluttonous** people end up **portly** and fat. If Jared ate half the food and became half the Jared, then where's the other half of the Jared? I had a **surfeit** of tacos, plus nine burritos, my favorite Mexican food? Ummm . . . Doritos. I'm a **gourmand**, fond of the food and the drink, sink piled with dishes, giving a **noisome** stink, a stinky stink, an annoying stink, a **noxious** stink, harmful and **baleful**. Speaking of stink, I had the **odious** task of cleaning all those dishes. The food was no longer **toothsome** and delicious. The odor was so **pungent** you could smell it down the block, **putrid**, **rancid**, and rotten, I had **forsaken** and forgotten. I get **somnolent** during the day, sleepy in daylight, wide awake and **vivacious** in the moonlight.

I do.
Yes and I do.
I do.

I like things that are cut short and **abbreviated**, like crew cuts, **aphorisms**, and speed dating. I've read Moby Dick, **abridged**, War and Peace, abridged, I found the writing to be so clear it was **pellucid**. Here's a piece of **acumen**, keen insight: there wouldn't be global warming if we all rode bikes. Here's a **maxim** to live by: do unto others as you would have them do unto you, too. Fulfill obligations, and be **dutiful**, act

infuse (v.) - to inject

quid pro quo (n., Latin) - a mutually beneficial exchange
gluttonous (adj.) - insatiable in appetite
portly (adj.) - fat, chubby, round

surfeit (n.) - an excess, a surplus, an overabundance
gourmand (n.) - one who likes eating and drinking
noisome (adj.) - foul, offensive, particularly to the sense of smell
noxious (adj.) - harmful, toxic
baleful (adj.) - harmful, threatening
odious (adj.) - meriting strong displeasure
toothsome (adj.) - delicious, luscious
pungent (adj.) - having a sharp, strong quality, especially related to smell
putrid (adj.) - rotten, rancid, foul
rancid (adj.) - rotten, spoiled, disgusting in smell or taste
forsake (v.) - to abandon, forget
somnolent (adj.) - sleepy
vivacious (adj.) - lively, spirited, full of life

abbreviate (v.) - to shorten, reduce
aphorism (n.) - a short saying
abridge (v.) - to shorten, cut down
pellucid (adj.) - clear
acumen (n.) - keen insight

maxim (n.) - a common saying of advice or virtue
dutiful (adj.) - obedient, compliant

cool, like my man Dizzee Rascal. **Captivate** the audience, capture their attention, don't return it, but **abduct** it, kidnap it, like a **henchman**. We're the opposite of **stagnate**, 'cause we've got flow, **stagnant** waters grow old with nowhere to go. **Torpid**, the opposite of a torpedo, moving so slow, that's why I switched into my Speedo. But I don't look good in a Speedo, who said that? It must have been my twin, my **doppelganger**, my copycat, **mimicking** me, going on **excursions** dressed like me, picnics by the sea, olives and sea breeze . . .

captivate (v.) - to hold the interest of, to gain the attention of
abduct (v.) - to kidnap
henchman (n.) - a trusted follower, goon
stagnate (v.) - to be idle, to be still
stagnant (adj.) - still, not flowing
torpid (adj.) - lazy, lethargic, moving slowly

doppelganger (n.) - a ghostly double of a living person
mimic (v.) - to imitate, to copy
excursion (n.) - a trip, an outing

I do.
Yes and I do.
I do.

I've wandered through the **tortuous** streets of Prague, those windy roads and confusing boulevards. At a wedding, I **surmised** who was the bride, figured out that she was the one standing by my side. I love marriage, and **espouse matrimony**, I support it like the cheese supports the bologna. I make **laudatory** comments and praise brides, but I had never seen this **euphoric**, and happy, **gay** bride. Someone had set me up, played a trick and a **ruse**, had gotten the two of us together but didn't introduce. Then we were jumping up and down, **cavorting** around, **carousing** all night long, partying, and getting down. Someone called the coppers, but they couldn't stop us, they **buffeted** us with their clubs, hit us like thugs. I love **bourgeois** weddings, they serve **lavish** dishes, always offer a choice between chicken and fishes. Usually not a **buffet**, though sometimes there

tortuous (adj.) - winding, twisted

surmise (v.) - to guess, infer, suppose

espouse (v.) - to support, or to marry
matrimony (n.) - marriage
laudatory (adj.) - admiring, praising
euphoric (adj.) - elated, overjoyed
gay (adj.) - happy
ruse (n.) - a trick

cavort (v.) - to frolic, leap, prance
carouse (v.) - to revel, to party

buffet (v.) - to strike, to pound
bourgeois (adj.) - middle class
lavish (adj.) - extravagant

buffet (n.) - a spread of food involving choices

is, in which case I get **bloated** from the free coleslaw, so **lethargic** and lazy that I can't even rap, more **corpulent** and fat than Rush Limbaugh.

I do.
Yes and I do.
I do.

bloated (adj.) - swollen, bigger than desired
lethargic (adj.) - sluggish, weary, apathetic
corpulent (adj.) - very fat

Synonym Matching: In the space provided, write the letter of the synonym on the right that corresponds to the word on the left.

1. Infuse _____
2. Portly _____
3. Noxious _____
4. Acumen _____
5. Espouse_____
6. Tortuous _____
7. Euphoric _____
8. Ruse _____
9. Lethargic _____
10. Pellucid _____

A. Corpulent
B. Happy
C. Clear
D. Inject
E. Trick
F. Lazy
G. Toxic
H. Insight
I. Winding
J. Support

Sentence Completions: Each sentence below has one blank, indicating that something has been omitted. Beneath the sentence are five words labeled A through E. Choose the word that, when inserted in the sentence, best fits the meaning of the sentence as a whole.

1. I could smell the _____ odor of putrid fertilizer as I drove through rural Nebraska.
A) Winsome
B) Noisome
C) Olfactory
D) Saccharine
E) Palatable

2. I often grow _____ while watching foreign films; reading subtitles can be
exhausting.
A) Vivacious
B) Nocturnal
C) Diurnal
D) Somnolent
E) Soporific

3. To impress his students, Mr. Roberts tended to speak in _____ language, saying things like, "FYI, he just needs some TLC."
A) Random
B) Pedantic
C) Abbreviated
D) Circuitous
E) Elongated

4. "That which does not kill you makes you stronger," is an example of one of Nietzche's famous _____.
A) Tomes
B) Tracts
C) Essays
D) Ruses
E) Aphorisms

5. There is an increasingly large population of people who claim to have been _____ by aliens and taken to another planet.
A) Usurped
B) Abducted
C) Vexed
D) Dispatched
E) Extolled

6. My _____ cat lies on the windowsill all afternoon, taking in the sun and dreaming about cat heaven.
A) Torpid
B) Vivacious
C) Boisterous
D) Lachrymose
E) Cordial

7. Captain Redbeard, a swarthy pirate, was known for his parrot "Pepe," who _____ every word the pirate said.
A) Demeaned
B) Coveted
C) Despised
D) Savored
E) Mimicked

8. Full of energy after signing their record deal, the euphoric band _____ until dawn.
A) Caroused
B) Wallowed
C) Pillaged
D) Reposed
E) Transgressed

9. The wedding guests showered such _____ gifts on us that we had almost too many nice presents.
A) Emollient
B) Lewd
C) Lavish
D) Gaudy
E) Atypical

10. My basset hound is so _____ he can hardly walk to his food bowl.
A) Svelte
B) Puerile
C) Agile
D) Euphoric
E) Corpulent

Reading Comprehension: Read the passage below and answer the questions based on the text.

Though today we might find them indispensable, plastic sandwich bags are a relatively recent invention. Before the wonderful plastic sandwich bag captivated the world's attention, most people lived rather torpid, stagnant lives, with little variation. Portly construction workers would complain that the sandwiches their wives had made for them that morning were too putrid to eat. Without a plastic bag, many of the sandwiches grew rancid in the paper bag, especially if the paper bag was stored near a source of heat. Consequently, many construction workers began showing fatigue, working at a torpid rate and acting generally lethargic. Once the plastic bag arrived, the world rejoiced that a toothsome sandwich could keep its flavor all day long.

1. According to the passage, which of the following did not occur before the invention of plastic bags?
(A) Construction workers found their sandwiches putrid.
(B) The populace led slow, boring lives.
(C) Sandwiches were less complex.
(D) Construction workers were lazier.
(E) Sandwiches grew rotten.

2. Together, the words "rancid" and "toothsome" in the passage are examples of:
(A) Antonyms
(B) Homonyms
(C) Synonyms
(D) Metaphors
(E) Rhymes

Flux

Word Bank

Wax	Rectify	Remiss
Wane	Recalibrate	Relish
Fluctuate	Amend	Savor
Flux	Redress	Vacillate
Aberration	Vicissitudes	Invariable
Albino	Undulate	Immutable
Aghast	Bide	Dutiful
Diminish	Antechamber	
Augment	Variance	
Static	Pittance	
Steadfast	Suffice	
Dynamic	Zeitgeist	
Espy	Mutability	
Illusory	Entity	
Precarious	Surreptitious	
Fickle	Physiognomy	
Capricious	Misogyny	
Lull	Monogamy	
Mercurial	Polygamy	
Protean	Uniform	
Malleable	Unilateral	
Gape	Unique	

Lunar cycles, we **wax** and we **wane**, we **fluctuate** and change, it's never the same, it's the alternation bringing all the **flux** to this game, we vary the variables, it's never the same.

Aberration is a deviation from right, an **albino** is a man whose skin is all white. So you can stand **aghast**, shocked, and amazed, while the moon waxes and wanes through various phases. When it wanes, you know the bright light is **diminishing**, and when it is waxing, it's **augmenting**. My life's not **static**; no it's not **steadfast**, it's **dynamic**, ever-changing and prone to blast. I **espy** with my own eye a sliver of moonshine, but it's **illusory**, I can barely see. My future hangs in the balance, it's **precarious**, lacking security, dependent on various conditions, so I embark on all types of missions. Listen, here's **fickle**: "What a charming performance! Actually I did not like that performance. On third thought I really enjoyed it!" That's what scientists call being **capricious**, it's when you keep changing your wish list for Christmas. . . . That was a **lull** in the song, but it didn't last long, 'cause nothing stays the same, get it? I'm **mercurial**, first I smile then I frown, my attitude is all just up and then down. I swear I change colors like a chameleon, I take on diverse forms like I'm **protean**. I'm **malleable**, like Play-Doh, easily shaped. The student rapped for the teacher, but the teacher just **gaped**.

Lunar cycles, we wax and we wane, we fluctuate and change, it's never the same, it's the alternation bringing all the flux to this

wax (v.) - to increase gradually in size or degree

wane (v.) - to decrease gradually in size or degree

fluctuate (v.) - to vary irregularly

flux (n.) - a state of constant change or a flow

aberration (n.) - a deviation from the expected course

albino (n.) - a person or animal without pigmentation in their skin

aghast (adj.) - struck by amazement or terror

diminish (v.) - to decrease or make smaller

augment (v.) - to increase or make larger

static (adj.) - not moving, being at rest

steadfast (adj.) - fixed or unchanging

dynamic (adj.) - characterized by continuous change or activity

espy (v.) - to catch sight of, glimpse

illusory (adj.) - deceptive, produced by an illusion

precarious (adj.) - dangerously lacking in security or stability

fickle (adj.) - characterized by changeableness, whimsical

capricious (adj.) - impulsive, unpredictable, subject to whim

lull (n.) - a relatively calm interval, as in a storm

mercurial (adj.) - quick and changeable in temperament

protean (adj.) - readily taking on various shapes or forms

malleable (adj.) - easily shaped or formed

gape (v.) - to open the mouth and stare stupidly

game, we vary the variables, it's never the same

We've got to **rectify**, **recalibrate**, and repair, revise, improve, fix, shape up, and get square. We must correct, adjust, reform, and scrub, **amend**, **redress**, put right, and straighten up. The **vicissitudes** of life, those ups and down, you're born naked, but soon you're wearing caps and gowns. Time flows in like waves, **undulating**. I **bide** my time in this **antechamber**, I'm just waiting for a **variance**, just a **pittance** would **suffice** of the spirit of the times, you know the **Zeitgeist**.

Mutability is the property that allows an **entity** to change just what it's going to be. If you follow me we could travel **surreptitiously**, don't believe me? Read my **physiognomy**, check my face. When it comes to choosing with whom you want to be, never mix **misogyny** with your **monogamy**. I don't know, but I imagine that **polygamy** for those who practice it could get kind of messy . . . I'd rather be with one person, **uniform**, **unilateral**, united, **unique**, exquisite, and unparalleled. If I were negligent with my rhymes, you'd think I was **remiss**, but I never was remiss with my missus. I **relish** her flavor, it's what I love to **savor**, my love doesn't **vacillate** neither does it waver. It's **invariable**, constant, and **immutable**, no permutation is suitable. I'm **dutiful**, fulfilling obligations, 'cause I am obliged to open up my eyes, and gaze at the sky, . . . it's quite beautiful.

rectify (v.) - to set right, correct

recalibrate (v.) - to readjust or make corrections to

amend (v.) - to change for the better, improve

redress (v.) - to set right or remedy

vicissitudes (n.) - the unexpected changes and shifts often encountered in one's life

undulate (v.) - to move in a smooth wavelike motion

bide (v.) - to wait, or remain in a condition

antechamber (n.) - a waiting room

variance (n.) - a difference between what is expected and what actually occurs

pittance (n.) - a very small amount

suffice (v.) - to meet needs

Zeitgeist (n.) - the spirit of the time

mutability (n.) - capability of change

entity (n.) - something that exists as a discrete unit

surreptitious (adj.) - done by stealthy means, clandestine

physiognomy (n.) - the art of judging human character from facial features

misogyny (n.) - hatred of women

monogamy (n.) - having only one spouse at a time

polygamy (n.) - having more than one spouse at a time

uniform (adj.) - unvarying, conforming to one principle

unilateral (adj.) - having only one side

unique (adj.) - being the only one of its kind

remiss (adj.) - negligent, exhibiting carelessness

relish (v.) - to take zestful pleasure in, enjoy the flavor of

savor (v.) - to appreciate fully, enjoy

vacillate (v.) - to sway from one side to another

invariable (adj.) - not susceptible to change

immutable (adj.) - not susceptible to change

dutiful (adj.) - careful to fulfill obligations

Do You Remember?

Synonym Matching: In the space provided, write the letter of the synonym on the right that corresponds to the word on the left.

1. Espy _____
2. Capricious _____
3. Bide _____
4. Remiss _____
5. Savor _____
6. Aberration _____
7. Surreptitious _____
8. Vacillate _____
9. Immutable _____
10. Augment _____

A. Negligent
B. Clandestine
C. Glimpse
D. Increase
E. Enjoy
F. Waiver
G. Whimsical
H. Wait
I. Deviation
J. Invariable

Sentence Completions: Each sentence below has one blank, indicating that something has been omitted. Beneath the sentence are five words labeled A through E. Choose the word that, when inserted in the sentence, best fits the meaning of the sentence as a whole.

1. The crowd stood _____ as the famous celebrity unbuckled his belt and mooned everyone.
(A) Aghast
(B) Tarnished
(C) Adept
(D) Bloated
(E) Adamant

2. Though he started with nearly $200, after shopping for a turntable and some records, Pablo's funds had _____ to five or six dollars.
(A) Merged
(B) Burnished
(C) Diminished
(D) Admonished
(E) Forged

3. Despite constant criticism, the president remained _____ in her policy of taking every other Tuesday off.
(A) Random
(B) Steadfast
(C) Inquisitive
(D) Perfect
(E) Munificent

4. The scary moment is not when you hear the thunder itself; it's the _____ between the lightning and the sound of the thunder that is so frightening.
(A) Munificence
(B) Lull
(C) Encore
(D) Touchdown
(E) Collusion

5. "So I'm moody and unpredictable!" the gnome told his friend. "Gnomes are supposed to be _____ !"
(A) Diminutive
(B) Pale
(C) Emollient
(D) Excellent
(E) Mercurial

6. One of the most frightening monsters of cinema history is the _____ Terminator 2, who could melt into the floor or disguise himself as a carton of milk.
(A) Protean
(B) Inimical
(C) Punctilious
(D) Affable
(E) Gregarious

7. What better embodies the current _____ than a couple walking in the park hand-in-hand, each one talking on a cell phone to a different person.
(A) Hurdle
(B) Zeitgeist
(C) Linchpin
(D) Inclination
(E) Harmony

8. The theory of evolution posits that over time most species demonstrate remarkable _____ when faced with the threat of extinction.
(A) Hubris
(B) Forage
(C) Scarcity
(D) Susceptibility
(E) Mutability

9. Many nineteenth century novelists studied the science of _____ and subsequently gave all of their villains crooked noses or warts.
(A) Physiognomy
(B) Philosophy
(C) Sodomy
(D) Psychiatry
(E) Botany

10. The new waiter _____ polished the silverware as his boss had instructed him to do.
(A) Soothingly
(B) Movingly
(C) Coyly
(D) Dutifully
(E) Callously

Reading Comprehension: Read the passage below and answer the questions based on the text.

Abraham Lincoln was not a politician so much as he was a person of strong morals who happened to hold a political office. He remained steadfast in his beliefs, even in the face of harsh criticism and threats. Amid a time of such upheaval and flux, with a civil war beginning and slavery tearing the nation apart, Lincoln wasn't fickle, didn't fluctuate in his opinions or vacillate between different positions. In fact, it was this unwavering strength that allowed him to attempt to rectify the terrible slavery situation in America. But Lincoln's death prevented him from finishing the job he started, and his successors never kept Lincoln's promise to give every former slave forty acres of land and a mule in an attempt to redress and make amends for the evils of slavery.

1. Which of the following best states the main idea of the passage?
(A) Abraham Lincoln was America's greatest president.
(B) Abraham Lincoln contributed to the end of slavery.
(C) Abraham Lincoln was a man of unflinching beliefs.
(D) The promises of Abraham Lincoln were only realized much later.
(E) Without the help of the army, Lincoln wouldn't have accomplished much.

2. Which of the following was not a reason that Lincoln succeeded in helping to end slavery?
(A) He was wise.
(B) He was a man of strong moral values.
(C) He was steadfast.
(D) He didn't waiver in the face of threats.
(E) He didn't change his position on issues.

Dr. Doctor

Word Bank

Salient
Sybarite
Voluptuary
Hedonist
Immaculate
Deluge
Inclination
Propensity
Tantamount
Incredulous
Novel
Deleterious
Frenetic
Grotto
Irascible
Malaise
Modicum
Neonate
Olfactory
Fortitude
Ominous
Portentous

Presage
Premonition
Volition
Predestination
Prestidigitation
Tenuous
Obfuscate
Purport
Feign
Vim
Vigor
Veracious
Erroneous
Fallacious
Histrionic
Melodramatic
Fabulist
Convalescence
Dearth
Rife
Luminescence
Lithe

Limber
Pique
Peregrinate
Innate
Penchant
Rustic
Morose
Mollify

It's true my most **salient** characteristic, my most notable trait is that I love to kick it. I'm a **sybarite** all right, my life's devoted to pleasure. I'm a **voluptuary**, the seven senses are my treasure. I'm from a great long line of **hedonists**, those who seek pleasure, lick wine from lips, so when I see a sky so blue and **immaculate**, spotless, perfect, I give thanks for it. I don't want to spend that day locked up in a classroom, unless it's a mad storm, a **deluge**, or monsoon. I have a natural **inclination**, a **propensity** to be free, I'm running through the fields and the trees. I'm so sick of florescent lights, it's **tantamount** to being actually sick. I told that to my doctor but he didn't buy it, he was **incredulous**, a nonbeliever, even though I was running a 101 fever. "That's a **novel** problem," I said. "A problem with a book?" He said, "A problem that's new so let me take another look." Leaves me shook, not to see the sun is **deleterious**, it causes injury and it leaves me delirious. After six hours in a room I get frantic and **frenetic**, I get freakier than circus freaks and I start to panic. In a **grotto** or a cave I always misbehave, I'm hot-tempered and **irascible** when I'm at a rave.

I can't think when the sun's shining bright outside . . .

Doctor, I feel some kind of **malaise**, a general unease and my mind's in a haze. I'm so sure, I don't have a **modicum** of a doubt that I'm too sick to leave this bed and go up out. I feel like a newborn infant, a **neonate**, the world looks new, and I don't feel great. I'm having some **olfactory** problems with my sense of

salient (adj.) - significant, conspicuous

sybarite (n.) - someone devoted to pleasure and luxury, a voluptuary

voluptuary (n.) - someone devoted to sensory pleasure and luxury, a sybarite

hedonist (n.) - one whose primary pursuit is pleasure

immaculate (adj.) - impeccably clean, spotless, pure

deluge (n.) - a great flood or something that overwhelms like a flood

inclination (n.) - a tendency, propensity

propensity (n.) - an inclination, preference

tantamount (adj.) - equivalent in value or significance

incredulous (adj.) - skeptical, disbelieving

novel (adj.) - strikingly new, unusual, or different

deleterious (adj.) - harmful

frenetic (adj.) - frenzied, hectic, frantic

grotto (n.) - a small cave or cavern

irascible (adj.) - easily angered

malaise (n.) - a vague feeling of discomfort

modicum (n.) - a small amount of something

neonate (n.) - a newborn infant

olfactory (adj.) - relating to the sense of smell

smell. Everything smells like waffles and I'm tense as well. I think I've got a fracture in my **fortitude**, I think my courage is breaking, and I'm not faking. I also think it's kind of **ominous**, a **portentous** sign that every time I try to rhyme my eyes start crying. I have this **presage**, a future-thought, a **premonition** that by two weeks from Friday I'll be no longing living, dead in the kitchen, keys in the ammunition. My doctor said, "If you die it's your own **volition**." You can exercise your free will, it's not **predestination**, and if it seems so it's just a **prestidigitation**, just a trick, just a sleight of God's big hands. It's just a **tenuous** argument with no substance. You're **obfuscating** the discussion," my doctor said. "You're adding irrelevant facts to screw up my head. You **purport** to be sick, you claim that you're ill, but you're **feigning**, faking, and that's the real deal."

I can't think when the sun's shining bright outside . . .

Now typically, doctor, I'm full of **vim** and **vigor**, Now I feel hung over, but I drank no liquor. Would it be a little quicker if you just stop all the talk, doc, call the paramedics or cops. I'm being honest, I tell you, I'm being **veracious**, I'm not lying, it's not **erroneous** and not **fallacious**. You know I don't engage in **histrionics**, I'm not **melodramatic** and I don't throw fits. I'm not a **fabulist**, these here are no fables, I flow on turntables, I scoop with no ladles. I just want to get better, want some **convalescence**, want to escape from schools and the basements. There's a **dearth**

fortitude (n.) - strength, bravery
ominous (adj.) - foreboding or foreshadowing evil, portentous
portentous (adj.) - foreboding or foreshadowing evil, ominous
presage (n.) - an omen
premonition (n.) - a presentiment of the future

volition (n.) - a conscious choice or decision
predestination (n.) - the concept of destiny or fate
prestidigitation (n.) - a sleight of hand
tenuous (adj.) - having little substance or strength
obfuscate (v.) - to render incomprehensible
purport (v.) - to present an intention that is often false
feign (v.) - to fake or pretend to

vim (n.) -vitality and energy, vigor
vigor (n.) - vitality and energy, vim
veracious (adj.) - honest, truthful
erroneous (adj.) - mistaken, incorrect
fallacious (adj.) - incorrect, misleading
histrionic (adj.) - excessively dramatic or emotional
melodramatic (adj.) - exaggeratedly emotional or sentimental; histrionic
fabulist (n.) - a teller of fables; a liar
convalescence (n.) - the gradual return to health after illness
dearth (n.) - a lack, scarcity

of sunlight in my daily life. I want the days of farmer 'cause his days must be **rife** with sunlight, full of **luminescence** and brightness. I become **lithe** and **limber** in the sun there's no tightness. You pull down those shades you **pique** my anger, you prick my finger, you start up the danger. I travel on foot so I **peregrinate**. My love of nature's natural so it's **innate**. I have a **penchant** for **rustic** walks up and down the coast. When I can't take a walk I get gloomy and **morose**. The only way that I could be **mollified** or appeased, is to tear the roofs off the schools and let us all free.

I can't think when the sun's shining bright outside . . .

rife (adj.) - abundant

luminescence (n.) - light from nonthermal sources

lithe (adj.) - graceful, flexible, supple

limber (adj.) - bending or flexing readily, pliable

pique (v.) - to provoke or to cause indignation

peregrinate (v.) - to travel from place to place on foot

innate (adj.) - inborn, native, inherent

penchant (n.) - a tendency, partiality, preference

rustic (adj.) - relating to country life

morose (adj.) - gloomy or sullen

mollify (v.) - to soften in temper

Synonym Matching: In the space provided, write the letter of the synonym on the right that corresponds to the word on the left.

1. Voluptuary _____   A. Limber
2. Deluge _____   B. Cavern
3. Grotto _____   C. Truthful
4. Presage _____   D. Sybarite
5. Fortitude _____   E. Sleight-of-hand
6. Prestidigitation _____   F. Courage
7. Vim _____   G. Dramatic
8. Veracious _____   H. Vigor
9. Histrionic _____   I. Flood
10. Lithe _____   J. Omen

Sentence Completions: Each sentence below has one blank, indicating that something has been omitted. Beneath the sentence are five words labeled A through E. Choose the word that, when inserted in the sentence, best fits the meaning of the sentence as a whole.

1. One of the _____ differences between Derek and Nate is that Derek is completely bald.
A) Discordant
B) Defiant
C) Ambiguous
D) Salient
E) Distorted

2. Long hours at the bowling alley after school had a(n) _____ effect on Suparna's schoolwork.
A) Amicable
B) Skeptical
C) Deleterious
D) Innocuous
E) Jovial

3. It only took a few negative words before Julio, a(n) _____ old cowboy, would start looking for a fight.
A) Endangered
B) Serene
C) Irascible
D) Erudite
E) Elated

4. Crotchety old Pierre didn't even feel a _____ of happiness when he learned that his neighbor had a new baby.
A) Discrepancy
B) Facade
C) Doubt
D) Rejection
E) Modicum

5. The looming thunderclouds certainly looked _____, especially for the TV meteorologist who had predicted sun all afternoon.
A) Dubious
B) Topographic
C) Ominous
D) Bovine
E) Inviting

6. The plumber, who believed seriously in _____, thought that God had hand picked him to fix people's toilets.
A) Hegemony
B) Predestination
C) Pulchritude
D) Pathology
E) Superstition

7. Since Claire couldn't remember the statistics to back up her point, her argument remained _____ at best.
A) Superfluous
B) Obsolete
C) Tenuous
D) Tacit
E) Flawless

8. He stayed up half the night reading, but whenever his father came by, Tyrone quickly turned off his light and _____ sleep.
A) Feigned
B) Obfuscated
C) Relished
D) Absconded
E) Loathed

9. He loved to _____, and made sure to walk from Philadelphia to New York City at least twice a year.
A) Cavort
B) Peregrinate
C) Innovate
D) Sojourn
E) Wonder

10. Rob liked all music, but he had a particular _____for the mariachi guitar.
A) Sagacity
B) Umbrage
C) Indignation
D) Acumen
E) Penchant

Reading Comprehension: Read the passage below and answer the questions based on the text.

A recent study purported that lack of daily exposure to sunlight is the leading cause of malaise among teenagers. The study quoted scores of students who argued that despite their innate propensity to be outside when it is sunny, many of their teachers not only kept them inside but even closed the blinds on these sunny days. One student noted, "I'm not hedonistic, but I need a little sun on my face." He demonstrated the deleterious effects of lack of sunlight by lifting his shirt and showing off his sickly, pallid abdomen.

1. According to the recent study, students feel sick due to:
(A) Boredom after school.
(B) An overabundance of daily sunlight.
(C) The amalgamation of sunlight and breezes.
(D) A dearth of exposure to sunlight.
(E) The fact that they are hedonists.

2. The word "innate" in the passage above most closely means:
(A) Natural
(B) Strong
(C) Lackluster
(D) Overwhelming
(E) Dutiful

Piece of the Pie

Word Bank

Firmament
Trite
Cliché
Reiterate
Permeate
Pervasive
Existential
Sedentary
Tranquil
Labyrinthine
Boisterous
Manifold
Conduit
Vocation
Vicarious
Familial
Aggregate
Exemplary
Ambivalent
Vacillate
Amorous
Amorphous

Nebulous
Abort
Placid
Repose
Revel
Salutation
Sordid
Repulse
Licentious
Judicious
Stupefy
Pithy
Empathetic
Sympathetic
Sympathy
Empathy
Inundate
Rife
Strife

Every piece of the pie of life is me, from the love songs and trees, to the SUVs. Find the roots the [they? that?] connect you to every living thing, like a link from your pinky to all the dead kings.

O brave o'er hanging **firmament**, O majestical roof, you're much more than the vapors that make up you. It might be a **trite cliché**, that doesn't mean that it's dumb, every atom in all of us was once in the sun. I'll **reiterate** it, repeat it, in case it snuck by, every piece of you is made out of the sky. If my love spreads out and **permeates** the globe, then the feeling is **pervasive**, everywhere you go. To be or not to be, that is the question, it's **existential** 'cause it has to do with existence. I'm **sedentary** right now, sitting by this window, meditating, feeling calm, feeling **tranquil**. This world is **labyrinthine** curvy like a snake and I'm trying to decide which path to take or if I even have a choice. I make noise and act **boisterous** just to raise my voice, like a chorus, as **manifold** people have before us.

Every piece of the pie of life is me, from the love songs and trees, to the SUVs. Find the roots the [they? that?] connect you to every living thing, like a link from your pinky to all the dead kings.

I hope this song is a **conduit** between you and me, like a pipeline of tight rhymes and communication. We listen for the ring of our calling, our **vocation**, I'm too far in the mountains, and I get no reception. I please my mother, don't live life through deeds of others, **vicariously** through actions of sisters and brothers. **Familial** like mothers and daughters, fathers to sons, we **aggregate** and gather like

firmament (n.) - the sky, the heavens

trite (adj.) - overused, hackneyed
cliché (n.) - a trite, overused expression

reiterate (v.) - to repeat
permeate (v.) - to spread out, to pervade
pervasive (adj.) - inclined to spread throughout

existential (adj.) - relating to existence
sedentary (adj.) - sitting
tranquil (adj.) - calm, serene, peaceful
labyrinthine (adj.) - intricate, mazelike

boisterous (adj.) - loud, energetic
manifold (adj.) - many

conduit (n.) - a pipe, passage, channel

vocation (n.) - one's work or professional calling

vicarious (adj.) - experienced through another's actions
familial (adj.) - relating to family
aggregate (v.) - to gather, amass

pigeons around breadcrumbs. I'd like to be the best example of me, **exemplary**, why do I act superficial and petty? I'm **ambivalent** towards how I feel to the Earth, I love it and hate it, I've **vacillated**, back and forth. My **amorous** feelings of love towards the world are **amorphous**, **nebulous**, with no shape or borders. I won't **abort**, give up this life, no matter how ill I feel, 'cause love turns like a wheel.

Every piece of the pie of life is me, from the love songs and trees, to the SUVs. Find the roots the [they? that?] connect you to every living thing, like a link from your pinky to all the dead kings.

The **placid**, calm surface of a puddle in the morning, or the rest and **repose** that you get when you're snoring, I **revel** in the early-morning sun on my forehead, like a **salutation** or greeting from life, however **sordid** or dirty I might see shanty towns on the TV, I might see people act in a way that **repulses** me, disgusts me. People who don't have morals act **licentiously**. If they'd just think first, they'd act **judiciously**. Sometimes I open my eyes, I'm astounded and **stupefied**, by the way some of these folks are living their lives. I guess Kweli was right with his **pithy** insight; we're all just hustling and bustling to get by. When I can relate to how you feel, I feel **empathetic**. When I feel bad for you, I feel **sympathetic**. I have **sympathy** for those who don't have toes, my three-toed gramps had empathy for those folks. I **inundate** and flood every part of my life, 'till it's **rife** and filled

exemplary (adj.) - serving as an example
ambivalent (adj.) - having contradictory feelings
vacillate (v.) - to go back and forth, fluctuate
amorous (adj.) - relating to or showing love
amorphous (adj.) - without shape or borders
nebulous (adj.) - indistinct, hazy
abort (v.) - to give up unfinished

placid (adj.) - calm, tranquil
repose (n.) - rest, sleep
revel (v.) - to enjoy
salutation (n.) - a greeting
sordid (adj.) - dirty
repulse (v.) - to cause disgust or distaste, or to drive back, repel
licentious (adj.) - amoral, lawless, lewd
judicious (adj.) - of sound judgment
stupefy (v.) - to astound
pithy (adj.) - succinctly meaningful
empathetic (adj.) - feeling another's pain as one's own
sympathetic (adj.) - compassionate
sympathy (n.) - an expression of pity for another, compassion
empathy (n.) - the experience of another's feelings as one's own
inundate (v.) - to flood
rife (adj.) - full, replete

with love to overcome the **strife**. I drew my bath, now I'll sit in it, every coin has an infinite number of sides, keep flippin' it . . .

strife (n.) - conflict

Synonym Matching: In the space provided, write the letter of the synonym on the right that corresponds to the word on the left.

1. Reiterate _____   A. Replete
2. Tranquil _____   B. Lewd
3. Repose _____   C. Rest
4. Repulse _____   D. Calm
5. Licentious _____   E. Flood
6. Stupefied _____   F. Conflict
7. Rife _____   G. Compassion
8. Strife _____   H. Repeat
9. Sympathy _____   I. Disgust
10. Inundate _____   J. Astounded

Sentence Completions: Each sentence below has one blank, indicating that something has been omitted. Beneath the sentence are five words labeled A through E. Choose the word that, when inserted in the sentence, best fits the meaning of the sentence as a whole.

1. The smell of sizzling bacon _____ the house on Sunday mornings, reaching my nose even when I was in the third-floor bedroom.
A) Captivated
B) Ameliorated
C) Permeated
D) Masticated
E) Nauseated

2. Despite the many losses they had suffered, there was a _____ feeling of triumph and togetherness throughout the locker room.
A) Juvenile
B) Superfluous
C) Tenuous
D) Placid
E) Pervasive

3. Mr. Piat had one of those _____ chuckles that brought a smile to everyone's face and that could be heard from across the street.
A) Boisterous
B) Tranquil
C) Intrepid
D) Sensual
E) Serene

4. I'm _____ about a lot of things; Coke vs. Pepsi, MTV vs. Vh1, Baseball vs. Football, I really can't decide.
A) Sagacious
B) Ambivalent
C) Steadfast
D) Immutable
E) Invariable

5. While Emily and Pedro were just buddies in Middle School, _____ feelings definitely began to blossom at the high school dances.
A) Inimical
B) Gregarious
C) Amicable
D) Pugnacious
E) Amorous

6. "_____ the mission," I screamed dramatically as our sled spun out of control toward a massive snowdrift.
A) Abort
B) Espouse
C) Despise
D) Parlay
E) Find

7. The sea was _____, like glass, as we headed out to pick up our lobster traps at 5:00 A.M.
A) Turbulent
B) Agitated
C) Placid
D) Aquatic
E) Fathomable

8. "Greetings and _____," proclaimed the small Martian as he strolled down the gangway of his flying saucer to greet us cordially.
A) Maledictions
B) Salutations
C) Hexes
D) Benedictions
E) Orations

9. I was downright _____ by the astounding scale of the Grand Canyon; it was more gigantic than I ever could have dreamed.
A) Mollified
B) Satisfied
C) Perplexed
D) Stupefied
E) Vexed

10. I have incredible _____ for those with sports injuries; I busted my knee in a tetherball tournament back in '69.
A) Sympathy
B) Disdain
C) Gratefulness
D) Leniency
E) Empathy

Reading Comprehension: Read the passage below and answer the questions based on the text.

Sedentary below a sycamore tree, Noa squinted her eyes and tilted her head back to gaze at the bright-blue firmament. A pervasive feeling of utter tranquility swept over her suddenly, and she sighed. Amorphous images of past loves, nebulous forms like souls without bodies aggregated before her mind's eye, and she reveled in their presence. Reposing under this ancient tree, Noa was overcome by the placidity of life, by the relaxed existential reality of most objects: rocks, trees, the wind. How labyrinthine are the paths that guide us through this world! How amazing!

1. The narrator in the passage above is:
(A) Unaware of Noa's thoughts.
(B) Vaguely aware of Noa's thoughts.
(C) Analytical towards Noa's thoughts.
(D) Keenly aware of Noa's thoughts.
(E) More interested in his own thoughts than in Noa's thoughts.

2. The phrase "relaxed existential reality" in the passage above most probably describes:
(A) The way it's so easy to relax when you are in nature.
(B) The way that objects are unaware of the bustle of human existence.
(C) The way that nature will always prevail.
(D) The way that people and nature are exactly the same on some level.
(E) The way that people fall asleep at night.

It's All Mathematics

*It's all mathematics. We add like addicts.
We subtract like taxes, multiply like rabbits.
We divide like axes. It's all mathematics.*

Now a **Polygon** is a shape, with a bunch of
sides you can't make a polygon out of just two
lines. If you got sides of the same length, then
you know it's on, what you're dealing with there
is a **Regular Polygon**. **Triangle** three sides,
three sides to every story in a love triangle, I'd
suggest you don't tangle. **Quadrilateral** has
four sides, the stage might have four sides, it's
proof that the stage show's live. **Pentagon** has
five sides, my eyes staring at the **Pentacle**,
the five-pointed star inside. Now it's a sextet
standing in **Hexagon** formation, six people,
six sides, mix stays live. **Heptagon** is the one
that everyone forgets, seven sides, seven sins,
so don't ever forget, ruled by the **Heptarchy**,
the seven-person government, the fun of it is
that I joined so now eight people running it.
Octagon with eight sides, octopus with eight
tentacles, octane gas has eight molecules. Nona
means nine, Strega Nona dressed to the nines.
The **Nonagon's** a polygon with nine sides.
Decimate comes from killing one in every ten.
Now it means to destroy or kill all of them. A
Decagon has ten sides, **Decimal's** a tenth-part,
Decimeter ten yards, listen now the hook's
gonna start . . .

*It's all mathematics. We add like addicts.
We subtract like taxes, we multiply like rabbits.
We divide like axes. It's all mathematics.*

Congruent is equal, like the congregation under
the steeple, 'cause no matter your religion all
people are equal. **Equidistant** is equally distant,
equally close, the Pacific is adjacent to the West
Coast. **Perpendicular** is two lines that form
ninety degrees, So they look like Xs, crossbones,
and Ts. **Parallel** is two lines that will not cross,
no matter how far they travel across the universe.
A **Plane** is 2-D, flatter than sheets and definitely,
when I say 2-D I mean flatter than concrete.
Painting pictures, on this geometric journey, I'm
your mentor. In a **Circle** every point is equidistant
from the center. So if we both eat the same donut
at the same time, and you start on your side
and I start on mine, we'll each eat through the
Radius, to the center where we get a Lady and
Tramp kiss. The distance from one side, through
the middle to the other side is the **Diameter**, so
never say die. **Perimeter**, distance around a
circle is 2 pi R. **Area** is pi R squared, how much
space is in there, do you care? Well I sure hope
you do or I'll be eating pancakes, and you'll be
eating Froot-Loops.

*It's all mathematics. We add like addicts.
We subtract like taxes, we multiply like rabbits.
We divide like axes. It's all mathematics*

Chapter 3: Guide to the Songs

This guide to the songs will lead you through each song on A Dictionary and a Microphone. It outlines the narrator, plot lines, themes, examples of figurative language, and cultural references that you'll find on each track. But we certainly don't intend for this list to stifle any creativity or originality on your or your students' behalf. Please use this guide in any way that you see fit.

1. Transformation

Narrator–Someone who loves hip-hop and is vaguely critical of "bookworms."
Theme–Transformation, metamorphosis, evolution.
Figurative Language–
". . . people crowd around like Jesus eating his last meal . . ." (Simile)
". . . vast, voluminous, exorbitant, extensive, extravagant collection . . ."
(Alliteration)
"You'll be the paragon of animals . . ." (Hyperbole)
References–
- Outkast is a popular rap group from Atlanta.
- Run D.M.C. is a famous eighties' hip-hop crew from Queens.
- Nostradamus was a popular nonreligious prophet who lived in the sixteenth century.
- Carrie Bradshaw is Sarah Jessica Parker's character on Sex and the City.
- Tony Danza is an Italian-American actor who starred in the sitcom, Who's the Boss?
- Leonardo da Vinci's The Last Supper (1498) depicts the apostles crowded around a seated Jesus.

2. Shakespeare is Hip-Hop

Narrator–A lover of the English language.
Theme–The malleability and adaptability of language.
Figurative Language–
"I forage through this language like I rummage for food . . ." (Simile)
". . . it's fertile and fecund, flipping free-styling flows for all my folks . . ."

(Alliteration)
". . . we're more abundant than sunrays on the radiant days . . ." (Hyperbole)
References–
- Toussaint L'Ouverture helped lead the great Haitian slave revolt in 1791.
- ". . . a cold flow by any other name . . ." derives from the Shakespearean line, "What's in a name? / A rose by any other name would smell as sweet." (Romeo and Juliet, Act 2, Scene 2)
- ". . . what wind from yonder window blows . . ." derives from the Shakespearean line, "But soft! What light from yonder window breaks?" (Romeo and Juliet, Act 2, Scene 2)

3. Adventures of Carlito

Narrator–A take-no-nonsense friend of Carlito, who knows his friend well.
Plot–Carlito, a shy, obsequious young man, is walking his puppy through Central Park when a old man accosts him and takes his dog. Carlito tells his friend (the narrator), who eventually helps him retrieve his dog.
Themes–Excessive submissiveness as weakness, strength as the ability to stand up for yourself.
Figurative Language–
". . . fortify like a fort . . ." (Simile)
". . . revenge, restitution, some payback, retaliation, and retribution." (Alliteration)
". . . I might leave you bereft of your esophagus . . ." (Hyperbole)
References–
- Judge Judy (Judith Sheindlin) is a judge who arbitrates disputes between parties on network TV.

4. Phobia

Narrator–An easily frightened young guy who lives in a tough neighborhood.
Plot–The narrator is scared to walk by a haunted house.
Themes–Fear, haunted spaces.
Figurative Language–
". . . I'm transparent like diaphanous screens . . ." (Simile)
"The austere appearance, bare, and bleak . . . I'm too scared to speak." (Alliteration)
References–
- Jimmy Page is the lead guitarist for Led Zeppelin.

5. Friends

Narrators–A guy recalling his childhood days. Someone praising his girlfriend. A guy complaining about his imaginary friend.

Themes–Friendship as supportive, the diversity of various friendships.
Figurative Language–
"Like a tiger full of tranquilizers, he's mostly benign . . ." (Simile)
" . . . affable and amiable, she's always acting conciliatory and agreeable."
(Alliteration)
References–
- Wesley Snipes helped fight terrorists on a plane in the film Passenger 57.
- The Energizer Bunny appears in commercials, drumming constantly, with the
motto: "still going . . . nothing outlasts the energizer."
- Guess Who? is a two-player guessing game made by Milton Bradley.

6. FLO+CAB

Narrator–A happy rapper.
Theme–The confluence of two things, two things becoming one.
Figurative Language–
"Like a boomerang we're back . . ." (Simile)
"There are copious connotations for every single word . . ." (Alliteration)
References–
- Heathcliff and Claire Huxtable are the happily married couple on The Cosby
Show.
- Iron Chef is a popular Japanese television show (with a new American spin-
off) that features chefs competing to cook tasty food in an hour.
- Beverly Cleary is a prolific author of books for children and young adults.
- BoyzIIMen was a singing group from Philadelphia featuring a 1990's version
of Temptations-like harmony.
- Art Garfunkel was a harmony-singing member of the folk-rock group Simon
and Garfunkel. He didn't play an instrument.
- The Concorde (SST) was a commercial passenger plane that flew at
supersonic speeds.

7. Myriad Operations

Narrator–A pathetic (slightly sleazy) guy with too much confidence, but not that
much self-esteem.
Plot–The narrator tries in vain to talk to a girl he meets in a taqueria (a casual
Mexican restaurant).
Themes–Changing personality traits for others, attraction.
Figurative Language–
"Shot me with a quick, cursory glance . . . caused a contusion, started bruising
. . ." (Metaphor)
" . . . my tongue was complicit in my mind's crimes like an accessory to murder
. . ." (Simile)
" . . . I was blushing exorbitantly, excessively." (Alliteration)

References–
- Elmo is a friendly, red-furred monster from Sesame Street.

8. I Do

Narrator–A playful, weird lover of food.
Plot–In the first verse, the narrator discusses food and his dirty kitchen. In the second verse, he shares his advice and introduces his twin "doppleganger." In the third verse, he suddenly finds himself standing at the altar at a wedding in Prague.
Themes–The playfulness, randomness of life, the enjoyment of food.
Figurative Language–
". . . I support it like the cheese supports the bologna." (Simile)
". . . moving so slow, that's why I switched into my Speedo." (Alliteration)
References–
- Jared Fogle, the spokesman for Subway, lost more than 200 pounds eating nothing but Subway sandwiches.
- Speed Dating is a form of organized "group" dating in which singles meet and talk for only eight minutes and then rotate to meet new people.
- Dizzee Rascal is a progressive rap artist from London.
- Rush Limbaugh is a conservative radio talk-show host.

9. Flux

Narrator–Someone contemplating the vicissitudes of life.
Theme–The only thing constant is change.
Figurative Language–
"I swear I change colors like a chameleon . . ." (Simile)
"We've got to rectify, recalibrate, and repair, revise . . ." (Alliteration)
References–
- Play-Doh is breadlike modeling dough, colored and designed for children's play.

10. Dr. Doctor

Narrator–A hedonistic student who is in love with sunlight.
Plot–A student wakes up on a beautiful day, feels sick because he knows he'll have to sit in a classroom. He goes to his doctor to try to convince him he is sick, but his doctor thinks his patient is trying to fool him.
Themes–Appreciation of nature and beauty, the divide between civilization and nature.
Figurative Language–
"You pull down those shades . . . you prick my finger . . ." (Metaphor)
"I get freakier than circus freaks . . ." (Simile)

"I'm not a fabulist, these here are no fables, I flow . . ." (Alliteration)
References–
- A rave is an all-night dance event featuring large crowds dancing to electronic music, often in an old warehouse.

11. Piece of the Pie

Narrator–Someone meditating on life.
Themes–The connectedness of all things, that both sides of every story and feeling are equally true.
Figurative Language–
"We listen for the ring of our calling, our vocation, I'm too far in the mountains, and I get no reception." (Metaphor)
"I revel in the early-morning sun on my forehead, like a salutation or greeting from life . . ." (Simile)
". . . the rest and repose that you get . . ." (Alliteration)
References–
- "O brave o'er hanging firmament," is from Shakespeare's Hamlet, Act 2, Scene 2.
- "To be or not to be," is from Shakespeare's Hamlet, Act 3, Scene 2.
- Talib Kweli is a rap artist whose 2002 single "Get By" posits that most people's actions come from doing the best they can to get by in this world.

Chapter 4: Hip-Hop Resources

The complete 10-Pronged Technique for Freestyle Rapping:
www.flocabulary.com/freestylerap

Interesting words and phrases that rhyme:
www.flocabulary.com/hiphop

Beats and instrumentals to rap over:
www.flocabulary.com/instrumentals

Freestyles, battles, and raps from emcees worldwide:
www.flocabulary.com/board

Freestyles & Metaphors

Freestyling

Freestyling is spitting words off the top of your head in real time. No rehearsal. No do-overs. Just off-the-top-of-your-dome lyrics to impress your girl or boy and keep your friends' heads bobbing. It is an art form of lucidity, feats of wordplay, and occasional, painful, mistakes. Here are a few things to keep in mind if you're looking to work on your freestyling.

* Listen to good hip-hop. One of the best ways to learn how to spit is to listen to the pros. Listen to the rhymes, write out the lyrics, rap along. Mos Def once promised that, "I spit lyrics so visual you can rent my rhyme books at your nearest home-video." We haven't found that store yet, but they do have his albums at the local library. Check out allmusic.com for great music info, and the Original Hip-Hop Lyrics Archive at ohhla.com for the lyrics of all your favorite artists.

* Practice. Practice. Practice. Even Big Boi sounded bad when he started. If you're just starting, you're probably going to sound bad, too. Just keep spitting! Spit during commercials, under bridges, and over breakfast. Flow in the shower, in your car, running around, with your friends. Rap over downloaded beats, instrumental tracks on CDs, or just over a song on the radio: blues, jazz, classical, hip-hop, whatever. Rap yourself to sleep at night.

* Rhyme. Start out easy, using "Doctor Seuss" vocabulary, and focus on rhyming. Work your way up to bigger words. As you practice you'll start to memorize rhyming pairs that you like, which you can use again and again. Some over-done examples are: devil/level, college/knowledge, making/bacon, hip-hop/tip-top, etc. You'll come up with your own favorites. I knew a sick emcee in Florence who liked to rhyme the word hurtles with ninja turtles.

* Finish the line. The real key to freestyling is to figure out in your mind what word you are going to end your first line with as soon as possible. As soon as you know this word, your mind should start racing to think up a word that rhymes (and is maybe somehow related) that you can use at the end of the next line. This is tricky, because even as you're spitting you need to be thinking about the cleverest, hardest, or most beautiful way to get to that word. For example, if you know that your first line is going to end with the word flapjacks, your mind should start choosing a rhyme even before you say flapjacks. Rhyme lists should quickly run through your head: map tax, chapsticks, packrats, backpacks. By the time you get to flapjacks, your second line should roll off your tongue like your last name.

It's outrageous, the way I flip the script like flapjacks,
You're trying to catch a free ride on my shoulders like a backpack.

Metaphors and Vocabulary in Hip-Hop

What we're doing with Flocabulary is novel, but it's also intimately connected with the evolving tradition of hip-hop music, which has always featured interesting wordplay, innovative metaphors, double-entendres, and examples of difficult vocabulary. Here are our top ten lists of great use of creative metaphors and of vocabulary. To add your own favorite to our online list, please go to:

www.flocabulary.com/hiphopmetaphors.

Our Nine Favorite Uses of Creative Metaphors and Similes

9. "See, I drop the greats like clumsy waiters drop plates
I got rhymes by the crates to erase the duplicates."
- Mr. Man on "Fortified Live," 2000 Seasons/Fortified Live 12
[Album Title OK as changed?]

8. "RRRRROAW RRRROAW like a dungeon dragon,
change your little drawers because your pants are saggin'."
- Busta Rhymes on "Scenario," The Low End Theory

7. "Coming from the deep black like the Loch Ness,
now bring apocalypse like the Heart of Darkness"
- Talib Kweli on "We Got the Beat," The Beautiful Struggle

6. "Like Slick Rick the Ruler I'm cooler than a ice brick,
got soul like those afro picks, with the black fist,
and leave a crowd dripping like John the Baptist,"
- Black Thought on "Mellow My Man," Do You Want More?!!!??!

5. "I'm cooler than a polar bear's toenails . . .
bend corners like I was a curve, I struck a nerve,"
- Big Boi on "Atliens," Atliens

4. "Me without a mic is like a beat without a snare . . .
I'm sweet like licorice, dangerous like syphilis."
- Lauryn Hill on "How Many Mics," The Score

3. "I come fresh like your breath after you brush,
wack mc's like that orange soda get crushed,"
- Fatlip on "The Pharcyde," Labcabincalifornia

2. "Throwing out the wicked like God did the devil,
funky like your grandpa's drawers, don't test me,
we're in like that, you're dead like Presley,"
- Q-Tip on "Steve Biko," Midnight Marauders

1. "My rhymes are like shot clocks,
interstate cops and blood clots,
my point is your flow gets stopped."
- Talib Kweli on "Hater Players," Mos Def and Talib Kweli Are Blackstar

Our Ten Favorite Uses of Big Vocabulary

10. "My rep grows like the nose of Pinocchio,
Just because I've mastered the art of braggadocio."
- Akrobatik on "U Can't . . ." The Lost Adats

9. "I gaze into the sky and measure planets by parallax,
check out the retrograde motion . . ."
- Wyclef Jean on "Zealots," The Score

8. "I'm known for causing spontaneous combustion,
constantly jumping through miscellaneous subjects,"
- Roscoe on "What I Look Like," Young Roscoe Philaphornia

7. "Holding my raps, Olden is golden and black,
extolling virtues of rap, with monkeys riding my back,"
- K-Os on "Emcee Murdah," Joyful Rebellion

6. "Dreams of euphoria, aurora, to another galaxy,
fallacy, be this microphone, but get lifted, lyrically I'm gifted."
- Lauryn Hill on "The Score," The Score

5. "Wes Jackson had the vision, and brought it to fruition
with a little hard work, perseverance, and intuition,"
- Aheru on "Soon Come," Soon Come

4. "Phased from your original plan, you deviated,
I alleviated the pain, with a long-term goal."
- Pharoahe Monch on "Simon Says," Internal Affairs

3. "We don't sell dope that you distribute,
we don't contribute to your clandestine activity,
my soliloquy may be hard for some to swallow."
- Andre (3000) on "Wheelz of Steel," ATLiens

2. "Claiming that you've got a new style, your attempts are futile,
oooh child, your puerile brain waves are sterile."
- Lauryn Hill on "How Many Mics," The Score

1. "You stopping us is preposterous like an androgynous misogynist,
you picking the wrong time, stepping to me when I'm in my prime
like Optimus, Transforming . . ."
- Talib Kweli on "Twice Inna Lifetime," Mos Def and Talib Kweli Are Blackstar

Chapter 5: Answer Key

Transformation

Synonym Matching	Sentence Completions	Reading Comprehension
1. B	1. E	1. D
2. F	2. C	2. B
3. I	3. E	
4. E	4. C	
5. A	5. E	
6. J	6. B	
7. H	7. D	
8. G	8. A	
9. C	9. C	
10. D	10. B	

Shakespeare is Hip-Hop

Synonym Matching	Sentence Completions	Reading Comprehension
1. H	1. C	1. B
2. E	2. E	2. B
3. C	3. A	
4. F	4. E	
5. I	5. B	
6. A	6. C	
7. J	7. E	
8. G	8. D	
9. D	9. E	
10. B	10. A	

Adventures of Carlito

Synonym Matching	Sentence Completions	Reading Comprehension
1. E	1. B	1. A
2. I	2. D	2. C
3. A	3. E	
4. C	4. B	
5. J	5. C	
6. F	6. A	
7. D	7. E	
8. H	8. B	
9. B	9. A	
10. G	10. D	

Phobia

Synonym Matching	Sentence Completions	Reading Comprehension
1. G	1. D	1. E
2. H	2. E	2. B
3. F	3. D	
4. E	4. C	
5. J	5. C	
6. D	6. B	
7. I	7. C	
8. C	8. A	
9. A	9. B	
10. B	10. C	

Friends

Synonym Matching	Sentence Completions	Reading Comprehension
1. I	1. C	1. B
2. E	2. E	2. D
3. J	3. D	
4. A	4. B	

Friends (cont.)

5. D	5. B
6. B	6. A
7. C	7. E
8. F	8. A
9. G	9. C
10. H	10. E

FLO + CAB

Synonym Matching	Sentence Completions	Reading Comprehension
1. D	1. C	1. C
2. F	2. E	2. E
3. H	3. B	
4. A	4. A	
5. I	5. D	
6. B	6. D	
7. C	7. B	
8. J	8. E	
9. E	9. A	
10. G	10. B	

Myriad Operations

Synonym Matching	Sentence Completions	Reading Comprehension
1. F	1. B	1. B
2. D	2. E	2. E
3. G	3. D	
4. B	4. C	
5. A	5. E	
6. C	6. A	
7. E	7. D	
8. I	8. E	
9. J	9. C	
10. H	10. B	

I Do

Synonym Matching	Sentence Completions	Reading Comprehension
1. D	1. B	1. C
2. A	2. D	2. A
3. G	3. C	
4. H	4. E	
5. J	5. B	
6. I	6. A	
7. B	7. E	
8. E	8. A	
9. F	9. C	
10. C	10. E	

Flux

Synonym Matching	Sentence Completions	Reading Comprehension
1. C	1. A	1. C
2. G	2. C	2. A
3. H	3. B	
4. A	4. B	
5. E	5. E	
6. I	6. A	
7. B	7. B	
8. F	8. E	
9. J	9. A	
10. D	10. D	

Dr. Doctor

Synonym Matching	Sentence Completions	Reading Comprehension
1. D	1. D	1. D
2. I	2. C	2. A
3. B	3. C	
4. J	4. E	
5. F	5. C	
6. E	6. B	

Dr. Doctor (cont.)

7. H	7. C
8. C	8. A
9. G	9. B
10. A	10. E

Piece of the Pie

Synonym Matching	Sentence Completions	Reading Comprehension
1. H	1. C	1. D
2. D	2. E	2. B
3. C	3. A	
4. I	4. B	
5. B	5. E	
6. J	6. A	
7. A	7. C	
8. F	8. B	
9. G	9. D	
10. E	10. E	

abase (v.) - to lower, demean, degrade

abate (v.) - to lessen, to reduce in severity

abbreviate (v.) - to shorten, reduce

abduct (v.) - to kidnap

aberration (n.) - a deviation from the expected course

abhor (v.) - to hate, loathe

abide (v.) - to put up with, tolerate

abject (adj.) - of the most miserable or contemptible kind

abort (v.) - to give up unfinished

abridge (v.) - to shorten, cut down

abrogate (v.) - to abolish, often by authority

abscond (v.) - to sneak away and hide

abundant (adj.) - in great numbers

accede (v.) - to agree

accentuate (v.) - to emphasize, to highlight

accommodating (adj.) - obliging, helpful

accost (v.) - to approach or confront aggressively

acumen (n.) - keen insight

acute (adj.) - sharp, severe

affable (adj.) - friendly, amiable

affluent (adj.) - rich, wealthy

aggrandize (v.) - to increase or make greater

aggregate (v.) - to gather, amass

aghast (adj.) - struck by amazement or terror

agoraphobia (n.) - an abnormal fear of open or public places

akimbo (adj.) - with hands on hips and elbows extending outward

alacrity (n.) - speed, readiness

albino (n.) - a person or animal without pigmentation in their skin

algid (adj.) - frigid, cold

allay (v.) - to soothe, assuage

alleviate (v.) - to relieve

aloof (adj.) - reserved, distant

altercation (n.) - an argument, dispute

amalgamation (n.) - a union, a merger

ambivalent (adj.) - having contradictory feelings

amble (v.) - to stroll, walk

ameliorate (v.) - to improve, to make better

amend (v.) - to change for the better, improve

amiable (adj.) - friendly, affable

amorous (adj.) - relating to or showing love

amorphous (adj.) - without shape or borders

anomaly (n.) - something that does not fit into the normal order

antechamber (n.) - a waiting room

anxiety (n.) - uneasiness

aphorism (n.) - a short saying

apocalypse (n.) - total devastation, the end of the world

apparitional (adj.) - ghostly, spectral

arbitrator (n.) - one who settles controversy between two sides

ascetic (n.) - one who practices restraint as a means of self-discipline, usually religious

assuage (v.) - to ease, pacify

atone (v.) - to apologize, make amends

audacious (adj.) - excessively bold

augment (v.) - to increase or make larger

austere (adj.) - very bare, bleak, simple

baleful (adj.) - harmful, threatening

bard (n.) - a poet, often a singer as well

battery (n.) - an assault or an array of similar things intended for use together

belligerent (adj.) - contentious, ready to fight

benevolent (adj.) - kind, good, caring

benign (adj.) - nonthreatening, innocuous

berate (v.) - to scold severely

bereft (adj.) - without, devoid of

bide (v.) - to wait, or remain in a condition

bilk (v.) - to cheat, to swindle

blandish (v.) - to coax through flattery

bloated (adj.) - swollen, bigger than desired

boisterous (adj.) - loud, energetic

bourgeois (adj.) - middle class

brash (adj.) - hasty or lacking in sensitivity

brazen (adj.) - excessively bold, brash

brumal (adj.) - wintry, relating to winter

brusque (adj.) - short, abrupt, dismissive

buffet (n.) - a spread of food involving choices

buffet (v.) - to hit or strike

burgeon (v.) - to come forth, blossom

cacophony (n.) - noise, discordant sound

cadence (n.) - rhythm

cajole (v.) - to urge, coax

callous (adj.) - harsh, cold, unfeeling

calumny (n.) - an attempt to defame

another's reputation

camaraderie (n.) - cheerful unity among a group

canvas (n.) - a piece of cloth on which an artist paints

capricious (adj.) - impulsive, unpredictable, subject to whim

captivate (v.) - to hold the interest of, to gain the attention of

carouse (v.) - to revel, to party

cavity (n.) - a hole

cavort (v.) - to frolic, leap, prance

celestial (adj.) - relating to the sky or the heavens

chastise (v.) - to criticize, to scold

choreographed (adj.) - arranged, as in dance

circumlocution (n.) - indirect language

circumspect (adj.) - cautious

clairvoyant (adj.) - able to see and detect things that others cannot

claustrophobia (n.) - an abnormal fear of closed or crowded spaces

cliché (n.) - a trite, overused expression

coalesce (v.) - to combine into one

cogent (adj.) - intelligent, viable

collusion (n.) - a conspiracy, a secret agreement

colossus (n.) - an enormous structure

comatose (adj.) - lethargic

commendable (adj.) - worthy of praise

commodious (adj.) - spacious, roomy

compel (v.) - to force

complicit (adj.) - being an accomplice in a wrongful act

compliment (n.) - an expression of esteem or approval

concede (v.) - to give in, to accept

conciliatory (adj.) - agreeable, friendly

concoct (v.) - to make up or invent

concord (n.) - agreement

conduit (n.) - a pipe, passage, channel

confluence (n.) - a convergence, a coming together

confound (v.) - to frustrate

connotation (n.) - a meaning or association suggested by a word beyond its definition

contusion (n.) - bruise, injury

convalescence (n.) - the gradual return to health after illness

copious (adj.) - abundant, plentiful

corpulent (adj.) - very fat

cosmopolitan (adj.) - worldly, sophisticated

credulity (n.) - readiness to believe

cursory (adj.) - brief to the point of being superficial

daft (adj.) - insane, foolish

daunting (adj.) - intimidating

dearth (n.) - a lack, scarcity

defame (v.) - to destroy the reputation of

deft (adj.) - skilled, adept

defunct (adj.) - no longer used or existing

deleterious (adj.) - harmful

delude (v.) - to deceive, to mislead

deluge (n.) - a great flood or something that overwhelms like a flood

derelict (adj.) - run-down, abandoned

desolate (adj.) - deserted, lifeless

despondent (adj.) - discouraged, hopeless, depressed

destitute (adj.) - impoverished

diaphanous (adj.) - transparent, light, airy

dictate (v.) - to pronounce, command, prescribe

differentiate (v.) - to distinguish, to make different

dilapidated (adj.) - in a state of disrepair

diligent (adj.) - careful, showing care

diminish (v.) - to decrease or make smaller

diminutive (adj.) - miniature, small

discreet (adj.) - prudent or inconspicuous

discrete (adj.) - separate, distinct, individual

disparage (v.) - to criticize, degrade, belittle

dissonance (n.) - lack of harmony or agreement

divergent (adj.) - different, deviating, contrary

diverse (adj.) - varied

divisive (adj.) - causing conflict, opposition

domicile (n.) - a residence, a home

doppelganger (n.) - a ghostly double of a living person

douse (v.) - to drench, saturate

dutiful (adj.) - careful to fulfill obligations

dynamic (adj.) - characterized by continuous change or activity

elocution (n.) - the art of public speaking

elucidate (v.) - to clarify

empathetic (adj.) - feeling another's pain as one's own

empathy (n.) - the experience of another's feelings as one's own

enervate (v.) - to weaken, make weary

enervated (adj.) - lacking energy, weakened, exhausted

entity (n.) - something that exists as a discrete unit

entomology (n.) - the study of insects

envious (adj.) - jealous

erect (v.) - to construct, to raise

erroneous (adj.) - mistaken, incorrect

espouse (v.) - to support, or to marry

espy (v.) - to catch sight of, glimpse

ethereal (adj.) - heavenly, exceptionally delicate or refined

euphoric (adj.) - elated, overjoyed

exacerbate (v.) - to make more violent, intense

excursion (n.) - a trip, an outing

exemplary (adj.) - serving as an example

exigent (adj.) - critical, urgent

existential (adj.) - relating to existence

exorbitant (adj.) - excessive

extol (v.) - to praise

extravagant (adj.) - excessive, over-the-top

fabricate (v.) - to invent, make up, concoct

fabulist (n.) - a teller of fables, a liar

facile (adj.) - easy

fallacious (adj.) - incorrect, misleading

familial (adj.) - relating to family

fatuous (adj.) - silly, foolish

fawn (v.) - to show affection through flattery

fecund (adj.) - fertile, fruitful

feign (v.) - to fake or pretend to

feral (adj.) - savage, wild, untamed

fetter (v.) - to restrain, chain, tie

fey (adj.) - magical

fickle (adj.) - characterized by changeableness, whimsical

figurative (adj.) - symbolic

firmament (n.) - the sky, the heavens

flabbergasted (adj.) - astounded, stupefied

flaccid (adj.) - limp

flattery (n.) - compliments, sycophancy

flout (v.) - to scorn, ignore, show contempt for

fluctuate (v.) - to vary irregularly

flux (n.) - a state of constant change or a flow

forage (v.) - to rummage, scavenge, graze for food

forestall (v.) - to delay, impede

forlorn (adj.) - lonely, hopeless

formidable (adj.) - arousing fear or alarm

forsake (v.) - to abandon, forget

fortify (v.) - to strengthen

fortitude (n.) - strength, bravery

fortuitous (adj.) - lucky, occurring by chance

foster (v.) - to stimulate, promote, encourage

frenetic (adj.) - frenzied, hectic, frantic

gape (v.) - to open the mouth and stare stupidly

gay (adj.) - happy, cheery, or homosexual

gilded (adj.) - covered with a thin layer of gold, or deceptively attractive

gluttonous (adj.) - insatiable in appetite

goad (v.) - to urge, to provoke into action

gourmand (n.) - one who likes eating and drinking

grandiose (adj.) - extraordinary, grand in scope

gregarious (adj.) - sociable, outgoing

grotto (n.) - a small cave or cavern

guile (n.) - deceitful actions or behavior

hail (v.) - to come from

hapless (adj.) - unlucky

harmony (n.) - agreement, often of sound

harrowing (adj.) - agonizing, distressing

hedonist (n.) - one whose primary pursuit is pleasure

henchman (n.) - a trusted follower, goon

hiatus (n.) - an interruption in continuity, a break

hiemal (adj.) - wintry, relating to winter

hierarchy (n.) - a ranking system of groups or individuals

histrionic (adj.) - excessively dramatic or emotional

idolatrous (adj.) - worshiping excessively an object or person

illusory (adj.) - deceptive, produced by an illusion

immaculate (adj.) - impeccably clean, spotless, pure

immutable (adj.) - not susceptible to change

impecunious (adj.) - excessively poor

impervious (adj.) - unable to be penetrated, unaffected

impudent (adj.) - rude, improper

incessant (adj.) - without interruption

incisive (adj.) - clear, sharp, direct

inclement (adj.) - stormy, bad, severe

inclination (n.) - a tendency, propensity

incredulous (adj.) - skeptical, disbelieving

indictment (n.) - accusation of wrongdoing

indignation (n.) - anger due to an unfair situation

inextricable (adj.) - hopelessly confused or tangled

infuse (v.) - to inject

ingenious (adj.) - marked by special intelligence

inimical (adj.) - hostile, threatening

iniquity (n.) - a wicked act, a sin

innate (adj.) - inborn, native, inherent

innocuous (adj.) - harmless

inquisitor (n.) - someone who asks questions or makes an inquiry

inundate (v.) - to flood

invariable (adj.) - not susceptible to change

invective (n.) - a verbal attack

inveterate (adj.) - habitual, natural

irascible (adj.) - easily angered

jubilant (adj.) - joyful, happy

judicious (adj.) - of sound judgment

juvenile (adj.) - young or immature

juxtapose (v.) - to put next to each other

labyrinthine (adj.) - intricate, mazelike

laceration (n.) - a cut, a rip

lachrymose (adj.) - tearful

latent (adj.) - present but hidden

laud (v.) - to applaud or praise

laudatory (adj.) - admiring, praising

lavish (adj.) - extravagant

lethargic (adj.) - sluggish, weary, apathetic

lewd (adj.) - vulgar, offensive, rude

libel (n.) - a statement that gives an unjust or unfavorable representation of a person or thing

licentious (adj.) - amoral, lawless, lewd

limber (adj.) - bending or flexing readily, pliable

limpid (adj.) - clear, easily understood

linchpin (n.) - something that holds separate things together

lithe (adj.) - graceful, flexible, supple

loquacious (adj.) - talkative

lull (n.) - a relatively calm interval, as in a storm

luminescence (n.) - light from nonthermal sources

magnanimous (adj.) - generous, noble

malaise (n.) - vague feeling of discomfort

malevolent (adj.) - having intent to harm others

malicious (adj.) - malevolent, harmful

malign (v.) - to slander, to smear, to libel, to defame, to speak evil of

malleable (adj.) - easily shaped or formed

mandatory (adj.) - required, not optional

manifest (v.) to show clearly

manifold (adj.) - many

masticate (v.) - to chew

matrimony (n.) - marriage

maudlin (adj.) - sentimental

maxim (n.) - a common saying of advice or virtue

meager (adj.) - lacking in quality or stature

mediate (v.) - to intervene, to arbitrate, to sort out

melodramatic (adj.) - exaggeratedly emotional or sentimental, histrionic

mendacious (adj.) - inclined to lie or mislead

mercurial (adj.) - quick and changeable in temperament

meritorious (adj.) - deserving of praise or merit

metamorphosis (n.) - a change of form, shape, substance

mimic (v.) - to imitate, to copy

misogyny (n.) - hatred of women

modicum (n.) - a small amount of something

mollify (v.) - to soften in temper

monogamy (n.) - having only one spouse at a time

mores (n.) - moral attitudes

morose (adj.) - gloomy or sullen

munificent (adj.) - generous, benevolent

mutability (n.) - capability of change

myopic (adj.) - short-sighted

myriad (adj.) - consisting of a very great number

narrate (v.) - to tell a story

nebulous (adj.) - indistinct, hazy

nefarious (adj.) - horribly villainous

neologism (n.) - the creation of new words, or a new word

neonate (n.) - a newborn baby

noisome (adj.) - foul, offensive, particularly to the sense of smell

notoriety (n.) - infamy, known in bad regard

novel (adj.) - strikingly new, unusual, or different

noxious (adj.) - harmful, toxic

obdurate (adj.) - unyielding to persuasion or moral influences

obfuscate (v.) - to render incomprehensible

obsequious (adj.) - excessively compliant or submissive

odious (adj.) - meriting strong displeasure

officious (adj.) - offering unwanted help or service

olfactory (adj.) - relating to the sense of smell

ominous (adj.) - foreboding or foreshadowing evil, portentous

oration (n.) - a dignified and formal speech

ostracize (v.) - to exclude from a community

pacify (v.) - to sooth, ease

paragon (n.) - model of perfection

pariah (n.) - an outcast

parody (n.) - a satirical imitation

patent (adj.) - clear, apparent

pedagogue (n.) - a schoolteacher

pellucid (adj.) - clear

penchant (n.) - a tendency, partiality, preference

peregrinate (v.) - to travel from place to place on foot

perfunctory (adj.) - showing little enthusiasm, done as duty

permeate (v.) - to spread out, to pervade

persevere (v.) - to persist, remain constant

pertinacious (adj.) - stubbornly persistent, holding to a belief or position

peruse (v.) - to examine carefully

pervasive (adj.) - spread throughout

petulance (n.) - irritability, impoliteness

physiognomy (n.) - the art of judging human character from facial features

pique (v.) - to provoke or to cause indignation

pithy (adj.) - succinctly meaningful

pittance (n.) - very small amount

placate (v.) - to soothe, appease

placid (adj.) - calm, tranquil

plethora (n.) - a great number, an abundance

pliable (adj.) - flexible, bendable

poach (v.) - to hunt or fish illegally

poised (adj.) - balanced, readied

polygamy (n.) - having more than one spouse at a time

portentous (adj.) - foreboding or foreshadowing evil, ominous

portly (adj.) - fat, chubby, round

precarious (adj.) - dangerously lacking in security or stability

predestination (n.) - the concept of destiny or fate

premonition (n.) - a presentiment of the future

preponderance (n.) - a great amount or frequency

presage (n.) - an omen

prestidigitation (n.) - a sleight of hand

presumptuous (adj.) - disrespectfully bold

profane (adj.) - indecent, blasphemous

profuse (adj.) - abundant, lavish, prolific

propensity (n.) - an inclination, preference

propriety (n.) - decency, state of being proper

protean (adj.) - readily taking on various shapes or forms

prudent (adj.) - cautious, careful

puerile (adj.) - immature

pugnacious (adj.) - belligerent

pulchritude (n.) - physical beauty

punctilious (adj.) - eager to follow rules

pungent (adj.) - having a sharp, strong quality especially related to smell

purport (v.) - to present an intention that is often false

putrid (adj.) - rotten, rancid, foul

quaint (adj.) - old-fashioned

quid pro quo (n., Latin) - a mutually beneficial exchange

quotidian (adj.) - daily, everyday

radiant (adj.) - bright, beaming

rancid (adj.) - rotten, spoiled, disgusting in smell or taste

ratiocinate (v.) - to think, contemplate

raze (v.) - to demolish

recalcitrant (adj.) - defiant

recalibrate (v.) - to readjust or make corrections to

recapitulate (v.) - to repeat, reiterate

rectify (v.) - to set right, correct

redact (v.) - to revise, edit

redoubtable (adj.) - formidable, commanding respect

redress (v.) - to set right or remedy

reel (v.) - to be thrown off balance or feel dizzy

refrain (v.) - to hold oneself back, forbear

reiterate (v.) - to repeat

relish (v.) - to take zestful pleasure in, enjoy the flavor of

remiss (adj.) - negligent, exhibiting carelessness

render (v.) - to say, or to make

renovate (v.) - to restore, return to original state

repose (n.) - rest, sleep

reprehensible (adj.) - deserving of criticism

repudiate (v.) - to reject, turn down

repulse (v.) - to cause disgust or distaste, or to drive back, repel

requisition (n.) - a demand for goods, often by an authority

restitution (n.) - compensation, reimbursement

retaliation (n.) - revenge, punishment

retract (v.) - withdraw

retribution (n.) - vengeance, revenge, payback

revel (v.) - to enjoy

rife (adj.) - abundant

ruddy (adj.) - having a healthy, reddish color

ruse (n.) - a trick

rustic (adj.) - relating to country life

saccharine (adj.) - overly sweet

sacrosanct (adj.) - sacred, holy

sagacious (adj.) - shrewd, showing sound judgment

salient (adj.) - significant, conspicuous

salutation (n.) - a greeting

sanguine (adj.) - cheery, optimistic, hopeful

sate (v.) - to satisfy (an appetite) fully

satiate (v.) - to satisfy excessively

savor (v.) - to appreciate fully, enjoy

scathing (adj.) - hurtful, critical

scourge (n.) - a plague

scurrilous (adj.) - crude, vulgar

sedate (v.) - to calm, soothe

sedentary (adj.) - sitting

seer (n.) - a fortune teller

seminal (adj.) - original, ground-breaking

serendipity (n.) - the act of finding things not sought, luck

slander (n.) - a false statement to damage the reputation of another

sobriety (n.) - moderation from excess, calm, tranquility

somnolent (adj.) - sleepy

soothsayer (n.) - a fortune teller

sordid (adj.) - dirty

spectral (adj.) - ghostly

spurious (adj.) - false but intended to seem believable or possible

stagnant (adj.) - still, not flowing

stagnate (v.) - to be idle, to be still

static (adj.) - not moving, being at rest

steadfast (adj.) - fixed or unchanging

strenuous (adj.) - requiring tremendous strength or energy

strife (n.) - conflict

stupefy (v.) - to astound

submissive (adj.) - easily yielding to authority

subsist (v.) - to live, exist

succinct (adj.) - marked by compact precision

suffice (v.) - to meet needs

supplant (v.) - to displace and substitute for another

surfeit (n.) - an excess, a surplus, an overabundance

surmise (v.) - to guess, infer, suppose

surreptitious (adj.) - done in a secret, or stealthy way

swarthy (adj.) - of dark color or complexion

sybarite (n.) - someone devoted to pleasure and luxury, a voluptuary

sycophant (n.) - a self-serving flatterer

sympathetic (adj.) - compassionate

sympathy (n.) - an expression of pity for another, compassion

synopsis (n.) - a summary

taciturn (adj.) - not inclined to talk

tantamount (adj.) - equivalent in value or significance

tedious (adj.) - boring, dull

telepathic (adj.) - capable of reading minds

tenuous (adj.) - having little substance or strength

terrestrial (adj.) - relating to the land

terse (adj.) - abrupt, short, brief

timorous (adj.) - fearful, timid

tome (n.) - a large book

toothsome (adj.) - delicious, luscious

torpid (adj.) - lazy, lethargic, moving slowly

torrid (adj.) - giving off intense heat, passionate

tortuous (adj.) - winding, twisted

tragedy (n.) - a disastrous event, or a work of art in which the hero meets a terrible fate

tranquil (adj.) - calm, serene, peaceful

travesty (n.) - a grossly inferior imitation

trek (v.)   to walk, travel by foot

trite (adj.) - overused, hackneyed

truculent (adj.) - eager to fight, violent

ubiquitous (adj.) - existing everywhere, widespread

ultimate (n.) - the last part, or a fundamental element

umbrage (n.) - anger, offense, resentment

uncanny (adj.) - of supernatural character or origin

undulate (v.) - to move in a smooth wavelike motion

uniform (adj.) - unvarying, conforming to one principle

unilateral (adj.) - having only one side

unique (adj.) - being the only one of its kind

upbraid (v.) - to criticize, scold, reproach

vacillate (v.) - to sway from one side to another

variance (n.) - a difference between what is expected and what actually occurs

variegate (v.) - to diversify

vast (adj.) - enormous, immense

veneer (n.) - a superficial or deceptively attractive appearance, façade

veracious (adj.) - honest, truthful

verbose (adj.) - wordy

vicarious (adj.) - experienced through another's actions

vicissitudes (n.) - the unexpected changes and shifts often encountered in one's life

vigor (n.) - vitality and energy, vim

vim (n.) - energy, vigor

vivacious (adj.) - lively, spirited, full of life

vocation (n.) - one's work or professional calling

volition (n.) - a conscious choice or decision

voluminous (adj.) - large, ample

voluptuary (n.) - someone devoted to sensory pleasure and luxury, a sybarite

wane (v.) - to decrease gradually in size or degree

wax (v.) - to increase gradually in size or degree

weather (v.) - to withstand or survive a situation

whet (v.) - to make more keen, stimulate

winsome (adj.) - charming, attractive

Zeitgeist (n.) - the spirit of the time

At Flocabulary, we know how difficult it can be to motivate students, to get them to connect with the subject matter. Having worked as tutors in Berkeley, Philadelphia and Boston, we've come to realize that you can lead students to a book, but you can't make them read it. The most fundamental step in teaching is getting students motivated to learn! Teachers can work hard to make the information clear, accurate, and interesting, but whether the students are going to learn it is ultimately up to them.

We had this in mind when we created Flocabulary. Flocabulary seeks not only to teach vocabulary words, but also to motivate and engage students. We want to encourage students to be passionate and to bring the things in their lives that hold their passion (music, art, relationships, creativity) into the classroom. We also want them to bring what they learn in the classroom out into the world.

We've fused hip-hop music with 500 challenging vocabulary words, and we always try to be engaging and creative in the music and lyrics. Whether we're mentioning Hamlet, making jokes about Iron Chef and Pokemon, or discussing how each atom in our bodies was once in the sun, we always seek to create lyrics that will engage students. We're trying to bridge the gap between the real world and the classroom, between Tupac and Shakespeare, between teaching and learning, between education and hip-hop.

We've designed a unique Free Language Arts Vocabulary Lesson Plan for bringing Flocabulary's A Dictionary and a Microphone into your classroom. We encourage you to mold the lesson plan so that it fits your class and your teaching style. Also check out our slant rhyme lesson plan, for discussing hip-hop and poetry together with slant rhyme.

We've also created a Teacher's Guide to the Songs that summarizes the plot, narrator, references, and figurative language in each song. Use this as a starting block for discussions or use it to clarify a line you don't understand.

Below you'll find some Frequently Asked Questions regarding hip-hop music and rap education. Please email any other questions to info@flocabulary.com.

Frequently Asked Questions

What is Hip-Hop?

Hip-Hop is a cultural movement born in the Bronx, New York in the late 1970's. At that time different cultural elements converged to form a new and dynamic urban art. Party DJ's were placing two turntables next to each other to mix and splice songs and were even beginning to manipulate the record by hand (scratching). MC's (master of ceremonies, i.e. the person with the microphone) would sometimes front for these DJ's, pumping up a crowd by rapping rhyming lyrics. Athletic dancers invented a new freewheeling dance style called break dancing. And graffiti artists were using spray cans to create enormous works of art on Subway cars and throughout the urban landscape.

Originally relegated to urban areas, hip-hop music has spread during the eighties and nineties, so that it now enjoys worldwide popularity. A truly global phenomenon, you'll find emcee crews in France, break dancers in Poland, DJ's in Pakistan, and hip-hop fans in rural Africa, urban Moscow, and suburban Tokyo.

Isn't rap music violent, sexist and profane?

While there is plenty of rap music that supports the unfortunate stereotype that hip-hop is always expletive-laced, violent, and derogatory towards women, there is also an enormous amount of hip-hop that is positive, beautiful, nerdy, eloquent, soft-spoken, weird, and funny. The more you probe hip-hop, the more you will find these elements in the music. Hip-Hop, in fact, is as diverse as life. There have been rap songs that are essays on inequality and the danger of drug use, meditations on violence and beauty, admonishments for corporate greed and keeping a proper diet, odes to lust and friendship, braggadocio-laced ego-trips, and nostalgic journeys through memory and time.

What is the difference between rap and hip-hop?

This question is tricky because it really depends on who you ask. To some people there is no difference. Others consider rap music just one element of the culture known as Hip-Hop (which also includes break-dancing, graffiti-writing, fashion, a way of talking, etc...). As one source notes, "Rap is what you listen to. Hip-hop is what you live."

What if I don't feel confident talking about hip-hop in my class?

We are well aware that you might not be a hip-hop scholar, that you probably didn't take a course in Old School Rap in graduate school, and that there will undoubtedly be students in your class that know a lot more about rap music and hip-hop culture than you do. Our advice is to use this fact to your benefit. Be honest with your class about trying something that you don't necessarily know a whole lot about. We suggest that you introduce Flocabulary to your students with a class discussion of rap music as it relates to poetry. This is a great opportunity for the students in your class who do know a lot about hip-hop to share their knowledge and feel empowered about what they do know. The goal of Flocabulary is really two-fold: teach kids SAT-levelwords, and also get kids motivated and confidant with the knowledge that this English language is theirs. The more empowered they feel with their knowledge, the more they will learn what you want them to learn.

If I had to buy three hip-hop albums to introduce myself to the music, what should I buy?

*Low End Theory - A Tribe Called Quest
*Mos Def and Talib Kweli Are Blackstar - Blackstar
*Aquemeni - Outkast

What if my question didn't appear in the list above?
You can email info@flocabulary.com. We'll do our best to answer any question on hip-hop education, rap or Flocabulary.

For more information and lesson plans designed for teachers and the classroom, please visit our teacher's webpage at our website: http://www.flocabulary.com/teachers.html

About the Authors

Blake Harrison and Alex Rappaport are avid fans of both hip-hop and words. A chance meeting in San Francisco led to the conception of Flocabulary. With Alex's penchant for eclectic hip-hop production and Blake's inspired lyrical weavings, beats and rhymes came together and Flocabulary, SAT-Level Vocabulary Builder was born. Blake honed his skills at the University of Pennsylvania, where he received a degree in English. Alex holds a music degree from Tufts University.

Ann Marie Mulready holds a Ph.D. from the University of Connecticut, where she also served as a graduate and undergraduate reading instructor and supervisor for preservice teachers. Dr. Mulready also has more than twenty-five years of classroom experience, serving as an English teacher and language arts consultant for both elementary and secondary programs.

Visit the Flocabulary website at www.flocabulary.com for more information about Flocabulary and sign-up for the electronic newsletter. Read more about special performances, appearances and speaking engagements by the authors.

Study Notes

Study Notes